SPECIAL
SERMONS
FOR
EVANGELISM

SPECIAL
SERMONS
FOR
EVANGELISM

by
GEORGE SWEETING

MOODY PRESS

CHICAGO

© 1982 by
THE MOODY BIBLE INSTITUTE
OF CHICAGO

Library of Congress Cataloging in Publication Data

Sweeting, George, 1924—
    Special sermons for Evangelism.

    1. Evangelistic sermons. 2. Sermons, American.
I. Title.
BV3797.S93S63 1982   252'.3   82-7999
ISBN 0-8024-8210-4   AACR2

Special gratitude is extended to Phil Johnson, who has assisted me in research and editing.

Contents

1

What Must I Do to Be Saved?

No one gets to heaven by accident! Although salvation is a gift, it is not something we simply acquire along life's way. No one ever drifted to heaven.

Jesus said, "Except a man be born again, he cannot see the kingdom of God" (John 3:3). What did He mean? Simply that unless each individual undergoes a life-transforming experience of salvation, he will not get to heaven. Salvation is a prerequisite to heaven.

Perhaps you are wondering, How can a person be saved? It is not a new question, but it is a question more relevant and more important to modern man than perhaps any other question. It was first asked on a dark night in a jail in ancient Greece, but it comes to us through the ages with the same ringing urgency.

In Acts 16 we read the account of the apostle Paul's ministry to the city of Philippi. Paul and Silas were conducting a series of meetings in that town. A young girl who was demon-possessed and had an ugly reputation followed Paul and his group around, calling out, "These men are the servants of the most high God, which shew unto us the way of salvation" (Acts 16:17).

Because this girl sanctioned the ministry and message of Paul, the people turned away in disgust. Paul knew that something had to be done, and it had to be done right away. So in the name of Jesus, he turned to the girl and commanded the unclean spirit to come out of her. Immediately she was set free.

But there was a group of men who made money from the girl because the demon gave her the ability to tell fortunes. When the demon left the girl, their business was destroyed. The men stirred up the multitudes against Paul and Silas, dragged them to the magistrates, and falsely accused them. Paul and Silas were severely beaten and cast into the inner dungeon in the Philippian jail.

Acts 16:25 tells us that Paul and Silas sang at midnight. They "prayed, and sang praises unto God: and the prisoners heard them." It was midnight, not normally the hour of prayer, but they prayed. It was a dungeon, not the normal place of prayer, but they prayed. They had been severely beaten, and you would think they wouldn't have felt much like singing, but they sang praises unto God. It was a dark, dismal dungeon, with no choir or musical accompaniment, but they sang praises unto God.

Prayer is always in order. Praising God is also appropriate. And the prayers and praises of Paul and Silas reached to heaven. God heard and answered their prayers. Their singing pleased Him, and He seemed to say Amen.

The Scripture says that there was an earthquake. The ground started to shake, and the doors were sprung. The bars were twisted, the chains fell off, and Paul and Silas were free.

The jailer awoke. He drew his sword and was about to commit suicide, knowing that he would have to pay with his life anyway at the hands of brutal authorities if the prisoners had escaped. But Paul and Silas were still there; and Paul, led by the Spirit of God, said, "Do thyself no harm, for we are all here" (v. 28).

Touched by the testimony of the power of their God and the reality of their compassion, the jailer "came trembling, and fell down before Paul and Silas, and brought them out, and said, Sirs, what must I do to be saved?" (vv. 29-30).

Now let's consider that question for a minute. Let us examine it from three different perspectives.

A PERSONAL QUESTION

First of all, the jailer's question was a personal question. "What must *I* do?" (v. 29). He correctly perceived salvation as a personal matter. God deals with us on a personal basis. He deals with us primarily as individuals, not as races, or as nations, or as families.

You may be a number in the eyes of the government or your employer, but you are a much-loved individual in the sight of God. He created you as an individual, He gave His Son to die for you as an individual, and He loves you as an individual.

Notice how God opened the jailer's eyes to his spiritual need. He was in an earthquake, his prison was damaged, and his life seemed in jeopardy. He was at the end of himself. He was ready to take his own life.

God often uses such circumstances to speak to a heart. Man's extremity is God's opportunity. And man's extremity is also man's opportunity. I have lived long enough to discover that moments of catastrophe and calamity often mark the beginning of a brand-new start.

Some time ago a soldier in a wheelchair came up to me. He said, "Dr. Sweeting, I was stricken with polio while in the military."

Naturally, I responded with, "I'm sorry."

"Oh," he said, "you don't have to be sorry. I'm glad God permitted me to be afflicted because it was in my despair that a fellow soldier related the claims of Christ. I heard the knocking of God through my affliction. I opened my life to

Jesus Christ. If I had never been stricken, I would not have sensed my need."

My friend, that is too often how it must happen. God must allow us to be stricken before we can see our need. Many people never see that salvation is a personal, individual issue that must be considered personally, individually by each one of us.

The Philippian jailer had to come to the point where his very life was in danger before he asked the question, "What must *I* do to be saved?"

But saying that salvation is a personal issue does not mean that it is a private one. The keeper of the prison certainly did not have the attitude that the state of his soul was no one else's business.

D. L. Moody once stopped a man on the street to ask if he had trusted the Lord Jesus as his personal Savior.

"That is none of your business!" answered the man.

"Oh, but it is my business," replied Mr. Moody.

"Then you must be D. L. Moody," the man said.

Yes, salvation is a personal matter, but not a private one. If you are a Christian, make it your business to lovingly confront men and women with the claims of the Lord Jesus Christ. Many people will never see the need for personal salvation unless we tell them.

Have you responded personally to the claims of the gospel? Have you personally put your faith in the Lord Jesus as the One who died for you, personally, on the cross? Salvation is not just for the down and out. It is for the up and in, the in and around, the good, the bad, the religious, the indifferent, the poor, the wealthy. It is for everyone. No matter who you are, you must be born again.

AN URGENT QUESTION

But also notice that the jailer's question was an urgent one. The question of salvation always is.

I notice that the apostle Paul did not say, "Let's talk about it when the excitement is over." Can you sense the urgency of the situation? A massive earthquake, widespread confusion, a suicide attempt, and an opportunity to escape the prison all contributed to the excitement. But the only thing crucial in the mind of the apostle Paul was the salvation of the jailer.

Some time ago a man spoke to me about receiving Christ as Savior. I had just concluded an evangelistic service, in which I had emphasized the urgency of the Bible's invitation to sinners to trust Christ. The man told me that he knew that he should receive Christ as Savior, but, he said, he did not feel quite ready.

I spoke with him kindly and lovingly and sought to challenge him to trust Christ then and there, but he repeatedly told me that although he was sure that what I was saying was right, he simply was not ready to receive Christ. He left without changing his mind.

But that man who was in no hurry to trust Christ was in too much of a hurry to get to where he was going. That same night, while driving at an excessive speed, he lost control of his car on a treacherous road. The car turned over and burst into flames, and that man perished that night. Earlier in the evening, he had told me that he was not ready to trust Christ. All I could think about upon hearing of his death was that he was not ready to die, either.

How I wish that I had talked to him a little bit longer! How I wish that I had pressed on him the claims of Christ just a bit further! But I learned one important thing from that incident, and I have never forgotten it. The message of the gospel is urgent!

I do not preach but that I think that there may be someone present who will never again have an opportunity to respond to the invitation of Christ. I do not share the gospel personally with a person but that I recognize the very real possibility that he may never again be confronted with the gospel.

D. L. Moody preached in a Chicago assembly hall on October 8, 1871. His message, as always, had an evangelistic theme, and he closed it by saying, "I want you to take home the question 'What shall I do with Jesus?' and come back next week with your answer."

Even as the service was closing, a commotion could be heard outside the building. People were shouting, and fire engines were moving through the street. The fire that was to destroy the city of Chicago was beginning to spread.

Many of the people in the service that night perished in the fire. There never was another meeting in that hall, and D. L. Moody learned one of the greatest lessons of his life. Never again did he close a message without pressing the congregation with the urgency of the gospel's claims. He never forgot that night of the fire when he had sent the people home to think about the gospel without giving an invitation for them to trust Christ then and there. And from that time on, his preaching was characterized by a sense of urgency that gave emphasis to everything he said.

My dear friend, delay can be dangerous. The road marked *tomorrow* leads to the town of *never*. Tomorrow is not God's time, it is the adversary's time.

The jailer in Philippi had no desire to wait. Delay was the farthest thing from his mind. "What must I do to be saved?" he asked, trembling. He was anxious to be saved. He had just been through an earthquake that might have killed him; he might have been killed for allowing prisoners to escape; and if Paul had not stopped him, he would have killed himself. He had perfect understanding that there is no guarantee of tomorrow. The only time that is certain is right now. His question was an urgent one.

But the question "What must I do to be saved?" is also a vital one. There is no hope for any man apart from salvation through the Lord Jesus Christ. The Philippian jailer was a man who had absolutely run out of hope. He was on the verge of suicide. He saw nothing to live for, and was prepared to end it all right there.

You may not be on the verge of suicide, but if you have never trusted the Lord Jesus and been saved, you know something of the hopelessness of life. No man can save himself. Human works are futile to produce genuine righteousness, "for there is none other name under heaven given among men, whereby we must be saved" (Acts 4:12).

Notice Paul's answer to the jailer's question. He did not say, "You are going to have to change your environment. You will have to get out of this jail and start going to church."

He did not say, "You are going to have to try to make yourself better. You must clean yourself up, change your image."

No, Paul simply pointed the man to the Lord Jesus Christ. "Believe on the Lord Jesus Christ, and thou shalt be saved" (Acts 16:31).

There are two ingredients in salvation: repentance and faith. The jailer had repented. His attitude and question to Paul were proof of that. He came as a broken, trembling, repentant man and asked the way of salvation. He was turning from his sin and selfishness and wanted to know where to turn. That is repentance.

Paul directed him to turn toward the Lord Jesus. That is faith. Faith is committing yourself to the Lord Jesus. It is trusting Him, casting yourself completely on Him.

That is vastly different from a mere academic faith. Paul did not tell the jailer to believe the truth *about* Jesus. Demons have that kind of faith, and that kind of faith alone cannot save.

Paul spoke of the kind of faith that believes "*on* the Lord Jesus Christ." That is faith that abandons itself completely to the object.

A minister was trying to lead an elderly Scottish woman to Christ. Try as he might, he could not seem to communicate to her the meaning of believing.

Leaving the woman's house he had to cross a small brook that flowed in front of the house. He paused at the rickety looking bridge and then gingerly touched it with a toe. The woman, sensing his hesitation, called out, "Can ye nay lippen the bridge?" which, translated from the Scottish dialect, means, "Can't you put your full weight on the bridge?"

He had just the expression he needed. Immediately he went back to the woman. "Can ye nay lippen Jesus?" he asked. Can't you cast your full weight upon Jesus? Can't you trust Him? Can't you commit yourself to Him?

With that expression the woman understood what it meant to believe. She trusted the Lord Jesus, and her life was changed.

My friend, God calls, but you must answer. There is something you must do to be saved, and that is to believe.

I asked a man the simple question, "Are you a Christian?" "No," he said, "I'm waiting for God to do something."

"God loves you," I replied. "Christ came into this world and died for your sins. When the Lord Jesus left this world, He sent the Holy Spirit, and He has called you and convicted you of your sins. God has done all that He is going to do. If you are ever to know God's salvation, You must respond. You must believe on the Lord Jesus Christ."

"What must I do to be saved?" Perhaps you are asking that question. The answer is the same for you as it was for the jailer at Philippi. You must believe on the Lord Jesus Christ. Will you do it today? You will never make a more important decision.

2

You Must Be Born Again

Yesterday a twenty-seven-year-old man sat in my office and said to me, "I am confused and mixed up. I have broken God's laws. I have lived contrary to His commandments. I thought I could get along without God. I made up my own rules, lived life my own way. But I failed. I would give anything to be able to go back, to start all over—to be born again."

I had the thrill of opening the Bible and sharing with him from God's Word about how he could indeed be born again.

According to John 3, the early ministry of Jesus attracted sensational attention, so much so that the Bible says, "Many believed in his name, when they saw the miracles which he did" (John 2:23). Nicodemus was one of those who had heard of the marvelous miracles the Lord was doing. He was a leader of the Jews, a respected teacher in Israel, and he came to the Lord Jesus at night, possibly to avoid detection.

Nicodemus began his conversation with a compliment and an especially wise observation. "Rabbi, we know that thou art a teacher come from God: for no man can do these miracles that thou doest, except God be with him" (John 3:2).

Nicodemus was very much like many people today who recognize Jesus as a great moral teacher, but do not see beyond that. The historian Klausner called Jesus the greatest moral teacher who ever lived, but nothing more! Others see him as a great religious leader, or as a teacher whose teaching methods were far ahead of His time.

But that is not enough. It is not enough to admire the Lord Jesus, or even to imitate Him. We must recognize that He is God and has authority to demand the right to be Lord of our lives. He is not simply a man, or even a great man. He is the God-man.

Jesus answered Nicodemus with a sledgehammer blow. "Verily, verily, I say unto thee, Except a man be born again, he cannot see the kingdom of God" (v. 3).

Born again? Perhaps your reaction is the same as Nicodemus's. He wondered how it was possible for a man to be reborn. Certainly it was not possible for a grown man to be born again in a physical sense. His mind was filled with questions.

Perhaps you have questions of your own about the new birth. I would like to examine four questions that people are asking today about the new birth.

WHAT IS THE NEW BIRTH?

What is the new birth? Look at Jesus' answer to Nicodemus. "That which is born of the flesh is flesh; and that which is born of the Spirit is spirit" (v. 6). The new birth is *a spiritual birth.* It has to do with a man's spirit, not his physical being. It is not a thing that can be observed with the eyes. Jesus said, "The wind bloweth where it listeth, and thou hearest the sound thereof, but canst not tell whence it cometh, and whither it goeth: so is everyone that is born of the Spirit" (v. 8).

The Lord was saying that the new birth is like the wind.

It cannot be seen or touched, but its effects are easily visible. That is because the new birth is *a new creating*. The apostle Paul put it this way, "Therefore if any man be in Christ, he is a new creature: old things are passed away; behold, all things are become new" (2 Corinthians 5:17).

And the apostle Paul knew all about it. Look at what we know of his life from the books of Acts. In 7:58 we see him as Saul of Tarsus, holding the coats of those who were stoning Stephen for his faith. In Acts 8:1-3, he is leading an attack against the church at Jerusalem. In Acts 9, he is on his way to Damascus when he is arrested by the Lord.

Saul became a believer, and his life was transformed. He was born again. He had a new allegiance and a new purpose. Instead of the greatest persecutor of the early church, he became its greatest missionary. His name was changed from Saul to Paul. Truly, all things became new; that is the essence of the new birth.

What is the new birth? It is *a passing from death to life*. Ephesians 2:1 says, "And you hath he quickened, who were dead in trespasses and sins." John 5:24 says, "He that heareth my word, and believeth on him that sent me, hath everlasting life, and shall not come into condemnation; but is passed from death unto life."

Sin kills. "For the wages of sin is death" (Romans 6:23). And every person is dead in his trespasses and sins until he is born again. The new birth brings life where there was death.

What is the new birth? It is *a calling out of darkness into God's light*. A few days ago I had the joy of leading a student to Jesus Christ. He said, "Dr. Sweeting, when I took the first step of faith in Jesus Christ, it was like a flood of light welling up in my life. My past was dark and foggy. Nothing was certain. Nothing was secure. But now I see. Things are clear. It is as if all the darkness in my life has been swept away by a spectacular light."

The apostle Peter wrote, "But ye are a chosen generation, a royal priesthood, an holy nation, a peculiar people; that ye should shew forth the praises of him who hath called you out of darkness into his marvellous light" (1 Peter 2:9).

The new birth, then, is a spiritual birth, a new creating, a passing from death to life, a calling out of darkness into God's light. The theological word for the new birth is *regeneration*. It all has a wonderful ring of newness about it, doesn't it? And that is what the Lord Jesus was saying to Nicodemus. All our old sins, the darkness of our hearts, the drudgery of our lives are replaced by a new, living, vibrant freshness. That is the new birth. It is a fresh start, a new beginning, a rebirth. Have you experienced that?

WHY DO WE NEED THE NEW BIRTH?

A second question you may be asking is, "Why do we need the new birth?" The Lord Jesus told Nicodemus that apart from the new birth a man will never see the kingdom of God. You see, there is something wrong with every man, something that can be supplied only by the new birth.

When a new baby is born, the doctors examine it very carefully and give each newborn a rating that is known as the Apgar score. Based on a scale of one to ten, the Apgar score rates an infant in regard to heart rate, respiration, reflex sensitivity, muscle tone, and color. A perfect score of ten is relatively rare, but it is not unheard of. But even those babies that receive a perfect Apgar rating have a defect that the Apgar score does not test for—a sinful nature.

The Bible is clear on the truth that all have sinned. Romans 3:10 says, "There is none righteous, no, not one." Verse 23 of that same chapter says, "For all have sinned, and come short of the glory of God." Isaiah wrote, "All we like sheep have gone astray; we have turned every one to his own way" (Isaiah 53:6).

Someone said concerning mankind, "Man has made great strides. He can swim like the fish and fly like the birds. Now he needs to learn to live like man." You see, all the greatest accomplishments of man—his art, music, philosophy; his great intellect; his scientific and medical discoveries; his laws and institutions; his architecture and engineering accomplishments; his religious and moral systems—all that combined has done nothing to lessen or eradicate the effects of sin.

Even the great Swiss psychologist Carl Jung said, "All the old primitive sins are not dead but just crouching in the dark corners of our modern hearts—still there, and still as ghastly as ever."

Look at any updated crime statistics and you will see that what Dr. Jung said is truer than ever today. Murder, rape, child abuse, incest, and even more hideous crimes are on the increase in our nation at alarming rates. Something is desperately wrong with mankind!

Political analyst Walter Lippmann commented several years ago, "We ourselves were sure that at long last a genertion had arisen keen and eager to put this disorderly earth to right—and fit to do it. We meant so well, we tried so hard, and look what we have made of it. We can only muddle in the muddle. What is required is a new kind of man."

Man has always tried to improve himself, but to no avail. What we need is indeed a new kind of man. And only the new birth can bring that about.

The Lord Jesus did not recognize class distinctions. He divided all the world into two groups: converted and unconverted—once-born and twice-born. *No* other divisions really matter. This is the decisive division; it is the division that runs through time and lasts for eternity. Into which division do you fit?

A third question commonly asked about the new birth is, "What will the new birth do for me?"

The new birth will *make you a member of God's family.* When you were born as an infant, you were born into a family. And unless you were adopted into another family, you took your name, your looks, and many of your characteristics from your mother and father. The same principles apply in the spiritual realm. When a person is born again, he is born into God's family. God is his Father, and he assumes the position and characteristics of a child of God. At first, he is a spiritual baby, but as he grows, he grows more and more into the likeness of his Father.

The only way into God's family is by birth. We do not become members of God's family by creation; it is a fallacy to say that all men are God's children. The apostle Paul, writing to the Christians at Ephesus, reminded them that, prior to their new births, they "were by nature the children of wrath, even as others" (Ephesians 2:3). He was saying that they were children of wrath, not children of God, until they were born into God's family; that is true of every man.

What will the new birth do for you? The new birth is a fresh start, a renewal. It will *renew your intellect and moral nature.* Colossians 3:10 reads, "And [you] have put on the new man, which is renewed in knowledge after the image of him that created him." In Ephesians 4:23-24 Paul wrote, "And be renewed in the spirit of your mind; And . . . put on the new man, which after God is created in righteousness and true holiness." A person who is born into God's family begins to assume the nature and mental and moral characteristics of God, his Father.

The new birth gives us a sensitivity to the things of God. The man who is born again seeks that which is pure (those things which are above—spiritual things). His affections undergo a transformation. He begins to love the things of

God—God's people, God's Word, and God's righteousness. His determination is different. His motives are changed, his desires are changed, his whole life is changed.

What will the new birth do for you? It will *make you the abiding place of God's Spirit.* When a man is born again, the Spirit of God takes up permanent residence in his body. Paul wrote to the Corinthian believers, "Know ye not that ye are the temple of God, and that the Spirit of God dwelleth in you?" (1 Corinthians 3:16).

Nothing can so transform a life as the complete surrender to the power of the indwelling Holy Spirit. Immediately there is a new authority in the life. The human will is conformed to the will of God. There is a new desire to do the will of God. The whole being is transformed.

HOW CAN I BE BORN AGAIN?

You may be asking, "How can I be born again?" The answer is surprisingly simple. "Believe on the Lord Jesus Christ, and thou shalt be saved" (Acts 16:31). Put your faith in Christ, trust Him completely, and you will be born again. There is nothing you can do to earn God's favor. Your works of righteousness are powerless to save you; they are like filthy rags in God's eyes (see Isaiah 64:6). You can no more obtain the new birth by your own efforts than an infant could be conceived and born through its own efforts.

"For by grace are ye saved through faith; and that not of yourselves: it is the gift of God: not of works, lest any man should boast" (Ephesians 2:8-9). Titus 3:5 says that it is "Not by works of righteousness which we have done, but according to his mercy he saved us, by the washing of regeneration [the new birth], and renewing of the Holy Ghost."

The new birth is a work of God. All we must do is trust Him completely. We must believe Him implicitly. We must put our faith in Him absolutely. Peter wrote that we are "born again, not of corruptible seed, but of incorruptible, by the word of God, which liveth and abideth forever" (1 Peter 1:23).

Has the seed of God's Word been placed in your heart? Do you see your need before God as a sinner? Do you long for a fresh start, a new birth, a regeneration?

The Lord Jesus died on the cross to make it possible for you to experience the new birth. He had never sinned; He did not deserve to die. But the Bible says, "For he hath made him to be sin for us, who knew no sin; that we might be made the righteousness of God in him" (2 Corinthians 5:21).

Christ's death on the cross was a payment for your sins. He paid the wages of sin—death—to make it possible for you to experience the abundant life He offered. But you must be born again. Will you trust Him today and experience that new birth?

3

Three Unpopular Sermon Topics

Not every subject in the Bible is pleasant. And one of the things that makes preaching the gospel such a challenging task is the responsibility in preaching the complete Word of God to deal with those topics that are not easy to preach about.

And yet the glorious truth is that for every negative there is a positive. For every unpleasant subject there is a victorious side—God has provided an answer to every problem mankind faces.

Today it is my task to speak on three sermon topics that are not popular. In recent years they have been neglected in many pulpits, yet they are vital in God's overall revelation to man. I would like here to examine what God's Word has to say about the subjects of sin, death, and hell.

SIN

Sin is virtually a forgotten word in the vocabulary of modern man. We talk about "personality disorders," "new morality," and "alternate life-styles," in our attempts to redefine what God's Word calls sin. We treat certain sins as sicknesses, without much success at finding a cure. Biblical standards are widely viewed as archaic, passé, and out-dated. Modern man has his own ideas, and they make no room for such a narrow concept as sin.

And yet there is no denying that the Bible teaches that sin is the real root of all of this world's problems. Denying the existence of the sin problem does not make it go away. Redefining moral values does little to remove guilt.

If you doubt that sin still exists, look at today's newspapers. Murder, war, prejudice, rape, theft, incest, child abuse, and other crimes and world problems fill the pages. And that does not take into account the secret sins that never make headline news, such as hypocrisy, covetousness, lust, and greed. Yes, my friend, sin is as alive as it ever has been.

And sin is a universal problem. There is not a man alive who is not affected by the problem of sin. Romans 3:23 says, "For all have sinned, and come short of the glory of God."

That verse gives a very important insight into the nature of sin. Sin is not, as some people think, only a heinous act, a vile thought, or a specific infraction of God's law. Sin is missing the mark, falling short of God's standards, coming short of God's glory.

That means that even the "good things" we do can be sin in the eyes of God. A remarkable verse in Isaiah says, "But we are all as an unclean thing, and all our *righteousnesses* are as filthy rags" (Isaiah 64:6, italics added). Do you see how God sees even our righteousnesses—the "good things" that we do? He says that they are as filthy rags. They miss the mark; they fall short of His glory.

The Lord Jesus, during His earthly ministry, had more conflicts with the Pharisees, the religious leaders of Israel, than with any other group of people. One of the reasons is that He exposed their hypocrisy for what it was—sin. He taught that their tithing and constant praying were of no value in obtaining God's favor. He called them whitewashed sepulchers, "full of dead men's bones, and of all uncleanness" (Matthew 23:27).

He openly exposed their secret sins. He showed them their shortcomings. He rebuked them for their phoniness. And He said that even the best things that they did were sin—their praying, their fasting, their tithing.

Does that mean that God is cruel or unreasonable? Certainly not. The Bible reveals God as a long-suffering, kind, loving, patient God. His standards are indeed high—too high for any man to attain. But God does not expect us to conquer the problem of sin by ourselves.

The answer to man's sin is in Christ. He is "holy, harmless, undefiled, separate from sinners" (Hebrews 7:26). He "did no sin, neither was guile found in his mouth" (1 Peter 2:22). He "was in all points tempted like as we are, yet without sin" (Hebrews 4:15).

And the Bible says, "Christ died for *our* sins" (1 Corinthians 15:3, italics added). His death on the cross for us made atonement for our sins. He paid the price to free us from our sins, and God raised Him from the dead, signifying that He had won the victory over sin!

The apostle Paul, writing to the believers at Rome, said, "Knowing this, that our old man is crucified with him, that the body of sin might be destroyed, that henceforth we should not serve sin" (Romans 6:6). And it is only through faith in the blood of Christ that we can experience that power to free us from our sin.

Are there sinful attitudes or sinful habits in your life that you long to be freed from? Is there sin in your past for which you suffer guilt and shame? The Lord Jesus Christ can free you from that, if you will trust Him unconditionally and put your faith in His work for you on the cross.

That is the good news about sin! We can be freed from its evil power, its guilt, its grip on our lives. We can be redeemed from the servitude of sin.

Another unpleasant subject that is often avoided in sermons is death. Death is a fact of life. We live with death every day. But we do not like to recognize death. The fear of death pervades our entire society. Anthropologists tell us that most adults never learn to face the fact of death honestly. As a result, millions of people die each year because they are afraid to see a doctor.

Death is all around us. The moment a man is born he begins to die. Billions of cells in the body are dying each day. The process of aging brings us ever closer to the inevitable time when we will die. Statistics show that two people die every second, 99 die every minute, 5,900 die every hour. Newscasts continually report deaths from natural disasters and the holocaust of war.

In this age of uncertainty, death is a sure thing!

In his letter to Christians, James spoke of the certainty of death. "For what is your life? It is even a vapour, that appeareth for a little time, and then vanisheth away" (James 4:14).

The Bible is clear on the certainty of death. Hebrews 9:27 says, "It is appointed unto man once to die." Death may not be a happy subject, but it is certainly an unavoidable one. Like it or not, everyone must die.

But that was not God's original plan.

When God created Adam He intended for man to live forever. Life was to be an endless adventure. Death was unknown. But Adam sinned, and the Bible says that because of Adam's sin, "death passed upon all men, for that all have sinned" (Romans 5:12).

W. Somerset Maugham wrote of an Arabian merchant who sent his servant to the city of Baghdad in search of provisions. The servant hurriedly returned, saying that he had seen Death in the marketplace and that Death had made a threatening gesture at him. He pleaded for a horse and hurriedly fled to the distant town of Samara, seeking to escape Death.

That day the merchant went to the marketplace. Seeing Death, he asked, "Why did you make a threatening gesture at my servant this morning?"

"That was not a threatening gesture," answered Death. "That was a start of surprise. I was astonished to see him in Baghdad, because I have an appointment with him tonight in Samara."

Death is inescapable. Scheme as you will, you cannot avoid your appointment with death!

The Bible is clear on the certainty of death, and it is also clear on the cause of death. The cause of death is sin. "The wages of sin is death," says Romans 6:23. Ezekiel 18:4 proclaims, "The soul that sinneth, it shall die." James concluded that "sin, when it is finished, bringeth forth death" (James 1:15).

People face death differently. One may die in confidence, another in despair. One may depart from this life in beautiful peace while another is racked by pain. One may die rejoicing while another is full of remorse.

Voltaire, the French philosopher and agnostic, declared when he was healthy that Christianity was a good thing for chambermaids and tailors to believe in, but not for people of wisdom. But before dying, he called to his doctor, "I am abandoned by God and man. I will give you half of what I am worth if you will give me six months of life. Then I shall go to hell, and you will go with me. O Christ! O Jesus Christ!" What a tragic way to die!

What a contrast is seen in the passing of John Wesley. This founder of Methodism is credited with saving England from moral disintegration during a critical time of that nation's history. It is said that without the ministry of John Wesley, England would have experienced the same kind of upheaval and decline France experienced in the revolution.

During Wesley's lifetime, he rode more than a quarter million miles on horseback and preached 42,000 sermons. When he lay dying at the age of eighty-eight, he said confidently, "The best of all is, God is with us."

Abraham Kuyper wrote, "In the valley of the shadow of death, the great highway divides itself. One road leads upward into eternal life and the other downward into eternal death, and Jesus Christ makes the difference."

Yes, my friend, Jesus Christ does indeed make the difference. Just as He is the remedy for our sins, He is the remedy for the problem of death.

Jesus said, "I am the way, the truth, and the life" (John 14:6). John wrote, "He that believeth on the Son hath everlasting life" (John 3:36). Are you fearful of death? The Lord Jesus said, "I am the resurrection and the life: he that believeth in me, though he were dead, yet shall he live: and whosoever liveth and believeth in me shall never die" (John 11:25-26).

Do you understand the importance of those words? Believers in Christ have nothing to fear in death. Our Lord has been victorious over death. Eternal life is ours now. We have it as a present possession. It is not merely something to look forward to, but a blessing to enjoy here and now. Our bodies may die. But real death will never touch us. We pass from this life immediately into the presence of the Lord Himself. Paul told the Corinthian believers that "to be absent from the body [is] . . . to be present with the Lord" (2 Corinthians 5:6).

And that is the good news about death. It is a defeated foe. It holds no threat for the one who has trusted Christ and received the gift of eternal life. Probably the most familiar verse in all of Scripture is John 3:16, and it is a simple expression of that very promise: "For God so loved the world, that he gave his only begotten Son, that whosoever believeth in him *should not perish, but have everlasting life*" (italics added).

Have you trusted Him and taken advantage of that promise?

HELL

Another unpopular subject is hell. A few years ago a major denominational magazine commented on the fact that hell is "going out of style for many contemporary believers." It gave statistics to show that fewer than one in three of that denomination's members really believed in a literal place of eternal punishment.

Hell today is a joking matter with many people. It is not uncommon to hear someone dismiss the concept of hell lightly with a comment like, "I suppose I'll feel right at home there—it is where all my friends are going."

But what a distorted and unbiblical view of hell that is! What ignorance is revealed in such a view! God warns us of hell primarily not to frighten us into obedience, but because He loves us. If hell genuinely exists, we would expect God to warn us of it. And He gives us abundant warning in His Word. The Lord Jesus spoke more about hell than He did about heaven! He lovingly and tenderly, but graphically, warned men and women of the horrors of hell.

To dismiss hell as an archaic and outdated concept is as ineffective in getting rid of it as that same approach is with the idea of sin. And to ignore hell will not make it go away any more than ignoring death makes it go away. No, my friend, like the unpopular topics of sin and death, hell must be squarely confronted and honestly faced. It is real, or else the Lord Jesus is a liar. It is real, or else the Word of God is not true. It is real if any other spiritual truth is real. We must admit that at the outset.

What do we know about hell? Actually, many things. It is a place, first of all, of eternal separation from God. Paul writes in 2 Thessalonians 1:9 that those who reject Christ "shall be punished with everlasting destruction from the presence of the Lord, and from the glory of his power." Those who refuse God's love and forgiveness here and now must spend eternity cut off from Him. Hell is separation from God.

It is also a place of suffering. Jesus gave a picture of the spirits awaiting judgment in the account of Lazarus and the rich man in Luke 16:19-31. The beggar Lazarus was in a place of joy after death, but the rich man, in hell, was in torment.

Again and again, Jesus emphasized the awfulness of hell and warned that it is unchangeable and forever. He called it "outer darkness." He used terms like "torment," "weeping and gnashing of teeth," and "everlasting fire." Hell must be an awful, horrible place.

You say, Can all of this be real? My friend, God does not play games with His creation. The Bible does not mix fantasy with truth. God would not give us such vivid descriptions of hell if it were not a real place with real suffering. He does not make idle threats.

The Lord Jesus said of heaven, "In my Father's house are many mansions: if it were not so, I would have told you" (John 14:2). The same thing is true of hell—if it were not so, the Lord Jesus would have said so. But instead He repeatedly warned of the awfulness of hell. He pleaded with people to escape the consequences of sin by believing and receiving eternal life.

But there is good news about hell. God does not want to send anyone to hell. Hell was not created for man but for the devil and his demons (Matthew 25:41). God is not anxious to send men to hell, but He is anxious to redeem them from it. That is not to say that no one will go to hell. Jesus taught that the road to destruction is broad and that many will travel that way. But the way to heaven is open to all in Christ.

The Lord Jesus died on the cross to redeem us from the

threat of eternal punishment. We do not have to go to hell. But He has done all that He can. The choice now is yours. Will you trust Him and receive His gift of eternal life, or will you reject Him and by your own choice be condemned to eternal punishment and torment in hell? Every man faces the choice sometime in his lifetime. You face it now. Will you trust Him or reject Him? Your choice will determine where you spend eternity.

Sin, death, and hell. None of them are pleasant topics, but all of them are real. And the Lord Jesus in His death on the cross has conquered all three. Will you trust Him today and know the joy and freedom that comes with eternal life?

4

Heaven and How to Get There

Every year, the little town of Pacific Grove, California, witnesses one of nature's spectacles. In the fall of the year, great clouds of orange and black monarch butterflies sweep down from the Canadian Rockies. They cluster on pine trees by the millions—to stay through the winter. In March, the butterflies fly off again, singly or in small groups. They drift widely, breeding wherever there is milkweed for their young.

After laying her eggs, a butterfly's work is complete. No butterfly makes the journey twice. Its life span is too short. But the next year, the offspring, who have never been to Pacific Grove, fly there to spend the winter. And each year, they arrive at exactly the same time!

How do the young butterflies know where to go? No one knows for sure. But their instincts guide them so directly that entomologists believe that the young butterflies return to exactly the same tree that their parents have come to for centuries. There is an inborn sense of direction and longing to return to the place of their ancestry in each butterfly.

In much the same way, God has planted within each man and woman a longing for a place called heaven. Romans 1 tells us that there is in every man an awareness of God. Paul writes, "That which may be known of God is manifest in them; for God hath shewed it unto them" (verse 19). And just like the butterfly that instinctively finds the right tree, so man instinctively directs his thoughts toward his Maker.

Man's inner consciousness of God has caused him to long for such a place as heaven. A study of the tombs of ancient Egypt tells us of the Egyptians' hope for the future. They believed in a future home that very much resembled what many of us conceive heaven to be like. The early American Indians also had belief in an afterlife in a place with the Great Spirit. Danish history reveals that, when a landowner died, his personal servant would also take his own life so that he could continue to serve his master beyond the grave!

In fact, virtually every civilization known to man has had an instinctive awareness of a future life. The instinct of heaven is registered in the soul. And man's soul needs such a place as heaven.

Perhaps you have unanswered questions about heaven. Most of us do. The greatest knowledge and intelligence that we can accumulate in this life is at best incomplete. We simply cannot come up with all the answers. In fact, the greater our knowledge, the more questions we have.

Isaac Newton was a brilliant English philosopher and mathematician, but he realized the limits of human wisdom. "I seem to be only a little child picking up a few pebbles on the shore," said Newton, "while a great ocean of truth stretches unexplored before me."

There really is very little that we know about our world here and now, and much less about heaven. But God's Word gives us some knowledge about this place to which every man longs to go. The truth the Scriptures give us about heaven is basic truth, but it is wonderful truth, and it answers some of the questions almost everyone wonders about.

How Can We Know There Is a Heaven?

One question the Bible answers for us is "How can we know there is a heaven?" The whole character of God demands that there be a place like heaven. God is *just*, and heaven is a place of reward for the righteous.

In a world racked by war and violence there is very little true justice. At times it seems that the wicked prosper at the expense of the righteous. And because evil continues to succeed here on earth, there must come a day when righteous judgment will be measured out.

Shall the wicked go unpunished? Shall the poor not be vindicated? Shall Jesus be crucified and not exalted? The answer from the Bible is a resounding no. Paul declared to the unbelieving people of Athens that God "hath appointed a day, in the which he will judge the world in righteousness by that man [Jesus Christ] whom he hath ordained" (Acts 17:31). And heaven is the reward of the righteous.

God is *merciful,* and His divine mercy demands that there be a heaven. God offers His forgiveness and salvation freely to those who will trust Christ. But what does that mean if there is no heaven and death ends it all?

When the Lord Jesus was dying on the cross, He told the repentant thief hanging next to Him, "Verily I say unto thee, To day shalt thou be with me in paradise" (Luke 23:43). The Lord promised that thief that, although he had spent a wasted life of sin, he could be redeemed and spend eternity in heaven. What a wonderful picture of the loving mercy of God!

God is *eternal,* and heaven is the place where we will spend eternity with Him. Paul wrote to the Corinthians, "For we know that if our earthly house of this tabernacle were dissolved, we have a building of God, an house not made with hands, eternal in the heavens" (2 Corinthians 5:1). Paul is saying that we have an eternal home where we will spend eternity with God.

God is *true,* so there must be a heaven. God would not mislead us on the subject of heaven. Our Lord said to His disciples, just prior to His crucifixion and subsequent resurrection and ascension, "In my Father's house are many mansions: if it were not so, I would have told you. I go to prepare a place for you. And if I go and prepare a place for you, I will come again, and receive you unto myself; that where I am, there ye may be also" (John 14:2-3). If heaven were not real, the Lord Jesus would have said so. But it *is* real, and He is there now, preparing a place for those who trust Him.

Yes, my friend, heaven is a real place. The Bible leaves no doubt about it. The Lord Jesus is there right now. Believers who die go to spend eternity there with Him. The reality of heaven is as sure as God Himself.

How Can We Know What Heaven Is Like?

But, you may be asking, can we possibly know what heaven is like? The Bible does give us some information about what heaven will be like.

The apostle John was given a glimpse of heaven one day in a beautiful vision. And he did his best to describe what he saw. We have it recorded in the Word of God in Revelation 21. In verses 18-19 of that chapter, John wrote, "And the building of the wall of it was of jasper: and the city was pure gold, like unto clear glass. And the foundations of the wall of the city were garnished with all manner of precious stones." The first verse of chapter 22 is part of the same account: "And he shewed me a pure river of water of life, clear as crystal, proceeding out of the throne of God and of the Lamb."

The God who painted the wings of the butterfly, who mixed the colors of the rainbow, who has painted nature with color and beauty—He is the Master Artist who has made heaven beautiful.

Yes, heaven is a beautiful place! It is a special place prepared for special people. It is a place of peace and rest and fulfillment. John tells us that in heaven "there shall be no night there; and they need no candle, neither light of the sun; for the Lord God giveth them light" (Revelation 22:5).

There is no sorrow there. "And God shall wipe away all tears from their eyes; and there shall be no more death, neither sorrow, nor crying, neither shall there be any more pain: for the former things are passed away" (Revelation 21:4). Can you imagine such a place? Surely there is no one who would not like to go to heaven.

HOW CAN WE KNOW HOW TO GET TO HEAVEN?

You may be asking, "How do I get to heaven? Can I know for sure that I will go there? Is it possible for *even me* to go to heaven?" You will be glad to know that the Bible does provide answers for those questions.

Several years ago, I thought I would like to find out exactly what the average man on the street thinks about how to get to heaven. I situated myself on one of the busiest intersections in the world—the corner of State and Madison streets in Chicago. As people passed by, I selected them at random to ask: "What are your chances of going to heaven when you die?"

Barbara, a high school senior, was the first person I questioned. "What are my chances of going to heaven?" she said. "I think my chances are very good. Not necessarily because of my own godliness, but because my father is such a good man. The Good Book says that we will meet our fathers in the next world. My father will be a saint, and I know he'll say a good word for me."

That young girl was very sincere, but very wrong. Being born in a Christian home does not make one a Christian. Basing your chances on a godly father and mother is very wrong. Godly parents may direct us in the right way, but they will not be able to "say a good word" for us to get God to accept us. Each of us is personally responsible to God.

The second person I questioned was a middle-aged businessman. "My chances of getting to heaven are pretty slim," he joked. "I can't play a harp, and I don't own any long white robes."

I meet people like that man all the time. They brush aside eternal matters with a silly remark, simply because they are not willing to confront reality.

We can speak carelessly of heaven and hell, my friend, but one day we will have to face their reality. Making light of eternal matters does no more to remove them than joking about the Grand Canyon could make it go away.

But the glib answer of that middle-aged man was only a cover-up. He was a man with a seeking mind. He promised to read the gospel of John that I gave him. Beneath his exterior of unconcern there was interest.

A young housewife was the third person I questioned. "How can I possibly tell about my chances of getting to heaven?" she asked. "You should ask my husband. He knows me better than anyone else."

I turned to her husband and asked, "What do you think of her chances of getting to heaven?"

"She has an excellent chance," he answered. "She lives a good life and is basically quite religious. I wish my own chances were as good."

As our conversation continued, it became evident that these young people were basing their hopes for heaven on their own good works, a good life, and a church relationship.

I was not surprised to find a couple that felt the way they did. As a matter of fact, I was not surprised by any of the answers I received that day. They represented a good cross section of the way people think about how to get to heaven.

But every answer I received that day was wrong, according to the Word of God.

No one gets to heaven by his own good works. If only good people went to heaven, there would not be anyone there! The Bible tells us that "all have sinned, and come short of the glory of God" (Romans 3:23). "There is none righteous, no, not one" (Romans 3:10). If we had to get to heaven on our own merits, none of us would make it! No one is righteous. No one can do enough good works to make up for his sin. It just does not work that way.

The apostle Paul wrote in Ephesians 2:8-9, "For by grace are you saved through faith; and that not of yourselves: it is the gift of God: not of works, lest any man should boast." Heaven and eternal life cannot be earned; they are gifts. They cannot be worked for or deserved. They cannot be purchased. They do not come to us because of our good works.

My friend, heaven is offered to you as a gift. It is offered freely, and the only way to get it is to receive it by faith.

Jesus said, "I am the way, the truth, and the life: no man cometh unto the Father, but by me" (John 14:6). No matter what you may have been taught, no matter what you may be doing to try to earn your way to heaven, the Lord Jesus says He is the only way to get there.

Think again for a moment of the thief on the cross next to the Lord Jesus. He did nothing to earn his way to heaven. He had lived a life of crime. He was being executed for his crimes, and by his own testimony, he deserved it. "And we indeed [suffer] justly," he told the other thief in Luke 23:41, "for we receive the due reward of our deeds."

He was repentant, but he was dying. He could not use his life to do good deeds. He had no opportunity to make restitution for what he had stolen. His life had been wasted. Completely. There was nothing left to salvage. Not even one day.

But our Lord promised the thief that that very day he would be with Him in paradise. He could be sure of it. It was the Lord's promise to him.

How did that dying thief get to heaven? The only way any man ever gets there—by faith. He trusted Christ. He put his faith in the Lord. He knew that Jesus was the promised Messiah. He knew that our Lord had done nothing worthy of death. And that thief committed himself to the Lord Jesus in his dying hours. "Lord, remember me," he asked (v. 42), and he was saved.

Will you commit yourself to the Lord Jesus in faith right now? What a tragedy to waste a life. You can reap some of the benefits of heaven right here in this life, if you will but trust Him. You can have eternal life. You can have the presence of the indwelling Spirit in your life. Have you trusted Him? If not, you need to be saved.

What must you do to be saved? Simply believe! What must you do to be lost? Nothing. Neglect is the same as rejection. Trust Christ as your Savior right now, and heaven will be yours.

5

Blessed Assurance

I heard a godly man say, "I'm as sure of going to heaven as though I had already been there a thousand years."

That is quite a powerful statement! Perhaps it is shocking to you to hear of someone so certain of heaven.

Uncertainty has robbed thousands of the joy of the Christian life. It is appalling to realize how many people are made miserable by the disease of doubt. Some people who read their Bibles, pray earnestly, attend church faithfully, and live uprightly in all their dealings with others may yet have no assurance of forgiveness and salvation.

Is it really possible to know for certain that you are going to heaven? What does the Bible say? Second Peter 1:10 tells us that we are to "give diligence to make [our] calling and election sure." God wants us to *know* that we are saved. Second Corinthians 13:5 exhorts us: "Examine yourselves, whether ye be in the faith." The Lord expects us to be certain. First John 5:13 says, "These things have I written . . . that ye may know that ye have eternal life." There is no question from the Scriptures that God's plan for us includes absolute certainty of our salvation.

Let me go a step further. Assurance is not only possible

but necessary, because it is the reality of assurance that brings purpose and power to our lives. Christian assurance is a fortress of strength against the wiles of the devil. But an uncertain salvation is impotent.

My friend, don't waste years in doubt—move forward to enjoy the greater things of God. Assurance may not be necessary for salvation, but it is certainly necessary if you would experience the victorious, vibrant, overcoming life.

Many people depend on their feelings for assurance, but feelings are no basis for genuine assurance. How you feel is certainly not the best measure of whether or not you have eternal life. Feelings have their place, but they are not the best barometer of your spiritual condition.

How can you be sure you are on your way to heaven? Let me suggest four issues in the matter of assurance that must be considered in the proper order.

FACTS

The first issue is the facts of the gospel. No one can be sure of his salvation until he understands the way of salvation.

What are the facts of the gospel? In his first letter to the believers at Corinth, Paul wrote, "For I delivered unto you first of all that which I also received, how that Christ died for our sins according to the scriptures; and that he was buried, and that he rose again the third day according to the scriptures" (1 Corinthians 15:3-4). That, according to the apostle Paul, is the essence of the gospel. Those are the facts of the gospel—that Christ died for our sins, was buried, and rose again the third day. Look carefully at three facts:

First, *Christ died for our sins according to the Scriptures.* When we think of the Scriptures we think of the Old Testament and the New Testament. But when Paul wrote this letter to the Corinthians, very little of the New Testament had been written. When Paul speaks of the Scriptures, he means the Old Testament Scriptures. Christ died for our sins according to the Old Testament Scriptures!

Perhaps you did not know that the Old Testament Scriptures spoke of Christ's dying for our sins. Centuries before the birth of Christ, Isaiah prophesied the suffering and death of the Messiah. That prophecy is recorded for us in Isaiah 53.

Verse 3 is a vivid account of the sufferings of our Lord at the hands of the mockers. "He is despised and rejected of men; a man of sorrows, and acquainted with grief: and we hid as it were our faces from him; he was despised, and we esteemed him not." Why was this One suffering? Isaiah tells us that it was for our sins. "Surely he hath borne our griefs, and carried our sorrows: yet we did esteem him stricken, smitten of God, and afflicted. But he was wounded for our transgressions, he was bruised for our iniquities: the chastisement of our peace was upon him; and with his stripes we are healed" (vv. 4-5).

The consistent teaching of the Old Testament Scriptures is that there *must* be an offering for sin. Sin must be atoned for before it can be forgiven. Blood must be shed. The Bible gave the nation of Israel detailed instructions for sacrificing lambs and other animals. But those sacrifices were only temporary. They were object lessons on the doctrine of atonement, "for it is not possible that the blood of bulls and of goats should take away sins" (Hebrews 10:4).

What was needed was a perfect, sinless, spotless man— the Lord Jesus. John the Baptist called Him "the Lamb of God, which taketh away the sin of the world" (John 1:29). He was the perfect sacrificial Lamb—the only one who could make atonement for our sins.

And that is why He died—to pay for our sins. That is fact number 1 of the gospel.

Paul says also that *He was buried.* Our Lord was put in a borrowed tomb, more a cave than the kind of grave we think of today. Isaiah 53 had foretold it. "And he made his grave with the wicked, and with the rich in his death; because he had done no violence, neither was any deceit in his mouth" (v. 9). Christ's death was not trickery. He was really dead—a Roman soldier made sure of that by piercing His side with a sword.

The Lord Jesus Himself foretold that He would be dead for three days. "For as Jonas was three days and three nights in the whale's belly; so shall the Son of man be three days and three nights in the heart of the earth" (Matthew 12:40).

But that is not the end of it. Fact 3 of the gospel states that *He rose again the third day according to the Scriptures.* Without the truth of the resurrection, the rest of the gospel is meaningless. Paul writes, "If Christ be not raised, your faith is vain; ye are yet in your sins" (1 Corinthians 15:17).

The resurrection is the basis for our eternal life. In that same great chapter on the resurrection, 1 Corinthians 15, Paul writes, "For since by man came death, by man came also the resurrection of the dead. For as in Adam all die, even so in Christ shall all be made alive" (vv. 21-22).

That fact is the very basis for assurance of our eternal life. Paul wrote in Romans 6:8-9, "Now if we be dead with Christ, we believe that we shall also live with him: Knowing that Christ being raised from the dead dieth no more; death hath no more dominion over him." The resurrection is God's proof to us that we have eternal life! What a fact! And that is a good foundation on which to base your assurance.

FAITH

A second issue to consider if you would know complete assurance of your salvation is the issue of faith. Facts can do an individual no good unless he exercises faith in them. Faith is a personal appropriation of the facts. Hebrews 11:1 says, "Now faith is the substance of things hoped for, the evidence of things not seen." Faith is all the proof you need.

Faith is simply taking God at His word, believing that what He says is true, and accepting it personally for yourself.

Here's an illustration. Imagine a prisoner being offered a pardon. He is so overwhelmed after reading the document of pardon that he is in a daze.

You ask him, "Have you been pardoned?"

"Yes," he says.

"Do you feel pardoned?" you ask.

He replies, "No, I do not; it is so sudden."

"But," you ask, "if you do not feel pardoned, how can you know that you are? You are not yet released from prison. You say you do not feel anything. How can you be sure you are pardoned?"

He points to the document. "This tells me so," he says.

That is faith. He believed and accepted the truth. He felt nothing, he had experienced nothing, but he knew that the document was true!

The Word of God is God's document of pardon to you. You can accept it by faith.

And by faith is the only way you can accept it. "For by grace are ye saved through faith," wrote Paul in Ephesians 2:8-9, "and that not of yourselves: it is the gift of God: not of works, lest any man should boast." There is no way you can *earn* God's salvation. But He gives it freely to those who accept it by faith.

FRUIT

A third issue in the matter of assurance is fruit. "I am the vine," said Jesus in John 15:5, "ye are the branches: He that abideth in me, and I in him, the same bringeth forth much fruit: for without me ye can do nothing."

If you are longing for assurance of your salvation; if you understand the facts of the gospel; and if you have received God's pardon by faith, the next issue to consider is the issue of fruit. Examine your life to see if the fruits of your faith are showing up.

What did the Lord mean by "fruit"? He meant attitudes and works in the life of the believer. Again, it is vital that we understand the proper order. Faith must come before fruit. Fruit is a natural result of faith.

Fruit does not grow by effort or through labor. Fruit grows naturally, and aside from giving it the right environment in which to grow, there is absolutely nothing you can do to make it grow faster or more abundantly.

Good works in the life of a believer are like fruit. Given the right environment, enough food, light, and air, they just grow naturally. They are fertilized through exposure to the Word of God; they receive light as we walk in the light, and they get their air as we let ourselves breathe the spiritual atmosphere that comes with a constant fellowship with God in prayer.

Good works in the life of an unbeliever, however, are manufactured, artificial fruit. God tells us in Isaiah 64:6 that those works of righteousness are like filthy rags. Works without faith are not fruit, but rags.

What are some of the fruits in the life of the believer? Galatians 5:22 gives us a list of *the fruit of the Spirit:* "love, joy, peace, long suffering, gentleness, goodness, faith, meekness, temperance." Here is a test: are those qualities evident in your life?

John wrote his first epistle to help believers struggling with the problem of assurance. In 1 John 5:13 he wrote, "These things have I written . . . that ye may know that ye have eternal life." And John gave several tests—fruit to look for in our lives as evidence that we have been truly born again.

One of his tests is *the fruit of obedience.* "And hereby do we know that we know him," John wrote in 1 John 2:3, "if we keep his commandments." Do you want to know if you really know God? Examine your life. Are you obedient to His Word? Do you love His Word, hunger for it, and obey it? That is evidence.

Another of John's tests is *the fruit of sound doctrine.* "Whosoever shall confess that Jesus is the Son of God, God dwelleth in him, and he in God" (1 John 4:15). Do you give to the Lord Jesus the high place that Scripture accords Him? Is your doctrine in line with the Scriptures and not just the teachings of man?

John's third test is *the fruit of love.* In 1 John 3:14 John writes, "We know that we have passed from death unto life, because we love the brethren. He that loveth not his brother abideth in death." Do you sense a bond of love with those who are believers in the Lord Jesus? Do you automatically have a feeling of kinship with those who trust Him? That, according to John, is evidence that you have passed from death unto life. That is a fruit of salvation.

FEELINGS

Have you examined the *facts* of the gospel? Do you understand and are you sure of what God's Word teaches about how to be saved—how to pass from death unto life?

And have you examined your *faith?* Do you trust Christ? Have you appropriated by faith His salvation for yourself?

Have you examined the *fruit* in your life? Is the fruit there—evidence from your attitudes, character qualities, and behavior?

Having examined those issues, we are now ready to deal with the issue of *feelings.* Feelings do have their place. When you first believed, you may or may not have felt different. Whether you did or not is not really important. But let me suggest three feelings that may be evidence of your salvation, assuming that all the other issues of assurance conform in your life.

The first is *peace.* In Philippians 4:7, the apostle Paul

writes about "the peace of God, which passeth understanding." There is a sense of peace that comes to those who do not concern themselves with personal needs but through prayer and supplication let their requests be made known to God (Philippians 4:6). It is a peace that passes understanding, a peace that keeps the heart and mind of the believer, regardless of outward circumstances, a peace that defies worries and cares. Do you know that peace? Until you experience genuine assurance you cannot know it.

A second feeling that might be helpful in the matter of assurance is *joy*. Joy is not happiness. Happiness can come and go, but real joy—the joy that is a fruit of the Holy Spirit—is not dependent upon circumstances. Paul wrote of rejoicing in the midst of tribulation. Have you experienced that kind of joy? Only true believers know it.

Confidence is a feeling that is closely related to assurance. How can we have confidence? Like peace and joy, confidence is a feeling that does not come from within. Its origin is not in us but in the Holy Spirit. Perhaps you did not know it, but it is one of the ministries of the Holy Spirit to assure our hearts that we are born of God. It is only He, ultimately, that gives assurance of our salvation. Romans 8:16 says, "The Spirit itself beareth witness with our spirit, that we are the children of God." First John 5:10 says, "He that believeth on the Son of God hath the witness in himself." That inner witness is the Holy Spirit.

God wants us to have assurance. The gospel is a "know-so" salvation. Millions have known this blessed assurance, and it is still available today.

Fanny Crosby wrote in the beautiful gospel song "Blessed assurance, Jesus is mine" (1873). Can you sing that with conviction?

It is not presumption or arrogance to be certain of eternal life; it is God's will.

What is your response? Are you sure of your salvation?

Will you examine the issues of facts, faith, fruit, and feelings, and be sure?

Perhaps you have had no assurance because you have had no basis for assurance. You have never trusted Christ, and you do not have eternal life. You need to receive Christ as your Savior today. You too can trust Him and know the assurance that the Lord makes possible in Christ and through His Holy Spirit.

6

All Things Are Become New

Several years ago, while waiting to board a plane, I became engaged in a conversation with a young man and his wife. After watching several jets shoot into the murky darkness, the young woman remarked, "I wish I could vanish into space just like that plane and begin my life all over again."

She was an attractive young woman, a woman of wealth and position, yet her life was filled with emptiness and regret. Why did she want to escape? Because the ugly hand of the past was spoiling the present.

Today there are millions who echo those words of despair. Perhaps you feel much like that young doctor's wife. I have good news for you. According to God's Word, everything in your life can be new and fresh and vibrant. Second Corinthians 5:17 says, "Therefore if any man be in Christ, he is a new creature: old things are passed away; behold, all things are become new."

What a wonderful truth! *All* things are become new! That is just what millions in the world are looking for. It is what that young woman was seeking. And the apostle Paul says any man can experience it in Christ.

Let me suggest three specific things that become new when a person is "in Christ"—when an individual becomes a believer.

A NEW START

First, the individual that puts his faith in Christ gets a new start. "Old things are passed away," says Paul. Would you like to get rid of some of the "old things" in your life? Your old sin, your old guilt, your old cares, your old defeats, all are passed away the moment you put your faith in the Lord Jesus.

There probably is no greater challenge to any man than the challenge of overcoming the weight of his sin. Everyone is faced with guilt, and different people try to handle it in different ways.

Some people try to escape it. Many try to drink away their gloom and guilt. Some seek release through drugs and narcotics. Some try to find a way out by fulfilling the lusts of the flesh. Others create their own private fantasies. Still others give themselves over to sexual perversions and deeper sin—anything to help them forget the misery of their everyday existence. But most of those things only compound the guilt and make the sense of emptiness and misery worse.

In my counseling over the years, I have found that most people do not have to be convinced of their sin. Our conscience condemns us. We cannot even meet the artificial standards we set for ourselves, much less the standards God has set.

The apostle Paul wrote, "I am carnal, sold under sin. For that which I do I allow not: for what I would, that do I not; but what I hate, that do I" (Romans 7:19).

Isaiah lamented, "Woe is me! for I am undone; because I am a man of unclean lips, and I dwell in the midst of a people of unclean lips" (Isaiah 6:5).

Job, a moral and upright man, confessed, "I abhor myself" (Job 42:6).

And God's Word agrees, "There is none righteous, no, not one" (Romans 3:10).

What we need is indeed a new start. And the Lord Jesus said that a new start is possible, even necessary. Speaking to Nicodemus, a great teacher of the Jews, the Lord said, "Except a man be born again, he cannot see the kingdom of God" (John 3:3).

Think of it! The Lord said that it is possible to be reborn—to begin life all over again.

Martin Luther described his experience like this: "When, by the Spirit of God, I understood these words, 'the just shall live by faith,' I felt born again like a new man; I entered through the open doors into the very paradise of God."

Why is a new birth essential? No other experience can give a man a completely fresh start. A new start is not found by moving to a new place. Thousands think that if they can just run away to California, or Florida, or to someplace far away, they will be able to experience a fresh start in life.

A new start cannot be found in a new marriage partner or a new job. Those things might change our outward circumstances, but they cannot really change us on the inside.

No, my friend, a new start cannot be found in a new state, a new mate, or a new slate. Only the new birth can truly give a man a new start. Only the new birth can free us from our sins. Only the new birth can impart to us eternal life, and make us pass from death to life. Only the new birth can give us a new heart, new desires, new life.

And this new start is to be found only in Christ Jesus. If any man be *in Christ,* he is a new creature. It is through faith in Him that we are born again.

Would you like to experience this new birth and have a new start? You need to turn a new direction—turn away from your sin to the Lord Jesus. That turning is called *repentance*. Repentance is simply a change of heart, a change of mind. It is turning from self and from sin and from self-righteousness.

The other side of repentance is faith. Faith is simply looking to the Lord Jesus, trusting that what he says in His Word is true and abandoning oneself completely to Him in complete confidence that He is able to do what He says. He can give a new start. He can make all things fresh and new. Will you trust Him to do it today?

A New Song

In addition to a new start, the one who trusts Christ gets a new song. For the child of God life can be filled with music. The victorious Christian life is a joyful, exuberant relationship with God. When we come to know Jesus Christ as our Savior, we have a reason to sing. He gives us a new song and puts gladness into our hearts.

God's servant David was a man who enjoyed music. As a boy he would play upon his harp while he tended his sheep. In later years, his music quieted the weary soul of King Saul as David strummed his melodies in the royal palace.

But not all of life was sweet for David. Like many of God's children, he experienced times of difficulty, opposition, and turmoil. In Psalm 40 we read of his distress. But despite David's problems, we see in that psalm the mighty hand of his God at work in his life.

Psalm 40:1-3 reads, "I waited patiently for the LORD; and he inclined unto me, and heard my cry. He brought me up also out of an horrible pit, out of the miry clay, and set my feet upon a rock, and established my goings. And he hath put a new song in my mouth, even praise unto our God: many shall see it, and fear, and shall trust in the LORD."

To know God is to possess a song in one's life. Salvation and song are inseparable. The joy of the Lord generates

[handwritten note in margin: More than a boom box in one's ear...]

54

music in the soul. When a person is in fellowship with God, he has a new song to sing.

When Martin Luther first translated the Bible into the language of the people, a marvelous thing happened. All of Europe began to sing the praises of God. The whole concept of music was tranformed from a dull, joyless chant to harmonious melody. From the Lutheran Reformation came many great hymns of praise that are still widely used in churches today.

Music is the natural result in the heart of one fully yielded to the Lord. Colossians 3:16 says, "Let the word of Christ dwell in you richly in all wisdom; teaching and admonishing one another in psalms and hymns and spiritual songs, singing with grace in your hearts to the Lord."

You don't have to be a musician to experience that song of grace, but you do have to be Spirit-filled. Song is the result of being filled with the Holy Spirit. Ephesians 5:18-19 says, "Be filled with the Spirit; speaking to yourselves in psalms and hymns and spiritual songs, singing and making melody in your heart to the Lord."

That new song is a song of praise. In Psalm 40, David expressed his gratitude to the Lord for delivering him from a miry, horrible pit. He could sing because he had been delivered by the Lord, and his song was a song of praise.

My dear friend, do you know anything of God's deliverance? Perhaps you too find yourself in sin's horrible pit, a slave to lust or obsessed with worldly possessions. You can find forgiveness and deliverance right now—right where you are. And it will be the basis for a new song.

I want you to notice something very interesting about the nature of David's new song. It was a blessing to other people. He did not keep it to himself. Oh, I do not mean that he sang it aloud to others, although he may have. But the key is that the song made such a difference in his life that it was visible to everyone. In verse 3 David says,

"Many shall see it, and fear, and shall trust in the LORD."

What did they see? Didn't David use the wrong words? Did he not mean that they would *hear* it? No. He meant not the song itself but the echo of the song in his heart, which was visible in his life. He had *become* a song.

Do people see your life as a song? That is God's purpose for your life. He wants not only to *give* you a new song to sing, but also to *make* you a new song to be seen.

Perhaps you know a believer like David—someone whose life radiates music, a new song. Just being around him brings new music into your life and strengthens your faith in the Lord and His power to change a life.

The Lord wants all of us to have that kind of testimony. And if we will surrender our lives to the control of the Holy Spirit, He will fill us with song.

D. L. Moody once heard Henry Varley say, "The world has yet to see what the Lord can do through a man totally surrendered to Him."

Moody's answer was, "By God's grace I'll be that man." And he surrendered his life to the Lord as fully as he knew how.

The Lord did use D. L. Moody, and He filled his life with music. Moody, although not a musician himself, had a deep appreciation for the value of songs and hymns and spiritual songs. He was the first evangelist to use music widely in his campaigns. And from his ministry and that of his associate, Ira Sankey, came some of the finest gospel songs ever written. Moody's ministry is largely responsible for scores of the songs still in our songbooks today. The Lord gave him a new song.

A New Strength

A third new thing available to every believer in Christ is a new strength. The apostle Paul wrote, "I can do all things through Christ which strengtheneth me" (Philippians 4:13).

56

Paul was not speaking there of physical strength, but of a spiritual strength, a strength of character, an inner strength that cannot be gained by natural means. It is a strength available only through Christ, but available to everyone who trusts Him.

Nehemiah told the people of Israel, "The joy of the LORD is your strength" (Nehemiah 8:10). The believer's new strength is closely related to his new song. The inner sense of joy and peace that comes from absolute surrender to the Spirit of God is a great source of strength.

But this new strength is centered in a Person—the person of Christ. Paul said, "I can do all things through *Christ*."

Do you see what that means? In Christ every believer has the power to do everything the Lord requires of him. The strength to live the Christian life comes not from within the Christian, but from Christ Himself.

Paul said, "I am crucified with Christ: nevertheless I live; yet not I, but Christ liveth in me: and the life which I now live in the flesh I live by the faith of the Son of God, who loved me, and gave himself for me" (Galatians 2:20). He wrote to the believers at Philippi, and spoke of the great desire of his heart: "That I may know him [Christ], and the power of his resurrection" (Philippians 3:10).

The real depth of the power of the Christian's strength can be comprehended in the realization that it is the resurrection power of Christ. The same power that enabled Him to rise from the dead is the power by which we can live our daily lives!

Think for a moment about the power of God that is available to the Christian. It is power that has been proved victorious over sin. It has been demonstrated to be more powerful than death. Surely the believer can do *all things* through Christ, who strengthens Him.

Paul concluded his epistle to the Christians at Ephesus with these words: "Finally, my brethren, be strong in the

Lord, and in the power of his might" (Ephesians 6:10). He went on to describe the spiritual battle that every believer knows and the weapons that are available to the soldier in the Lord's army. But the most exciting thing in that whole passage is this assurance in verse 10 that the power for the battle is the Lord's power. It is *His* strength, *His* might, *His* energy. It is the same power that already has conquered the enemy.

Trusting in that power, no Christian can be defeated. Satan cannot be victorious. The resurrection power of Christ cannot be overcome.

Are all things new in your life? Have you experienced a new start? Are you singing a new song? Are you living in new strength?

You know the needs in your life. The answer to them is found in Christ. He can make all things new. Will you trust Him today and let His resurrection power work in your life?

7

Three Kinds of Repentance

In 1927, Charles Lindberg became a national hero by flying alone across the Atlantic Ocean. During that historic flight, his plane, *The Spirit of St. Louis,* traveled at an altitude of four thousand feet and at a speed of one hundred miles per hour.

Today, supersonic jets can fly fifty thousand feet in the air and streak across the sky at more than fifteen hundred miles an hour.

In 1896, the electronic genius Marconi established the first wireless radio transmitter. With his unique invention he was able to send and receive a signal over a distance of two miles, and the age of mass communications was born.

Today, via satellites, a visual and audible signal can be transmitted live worldwide, and we have even seen live color television pictures from the moon!

This is an era of unparalleled technological achievement. You and I have seen more change in our lifetimes than all of mankind has before us!

However, in this era of change, there are some things that, unfortunately, have not changed. Mankind has not known real peace in our lifetime. Millions of people live in a constant struggle, trying to find meaning in a fast-changing world, and seeking release from the guilt of sin.

Each year in the United States, fifty million people change their places of residence. Some statistics indicate that there is now one divorce for every three marriages. Mate-swapping clubs have become quite popular in many of our nation's cities and suburbs. Narcotics arrests in one state alone have increased by two thousand times in just ten years. Clearly, people are not statisfied, and they are looking for change anywhere they can find it.

The Bible tells us that the basic need of every man is the need for a spiritual change. In Luke 13:3 Jesus said, "Except ye repent, ye shall all likewise perish." *Repent or perish;* that is the option. You may try to change your place of employment, your residence, or even your mate, but those are merely changes of surroundings. Until you repent of your sins and experience salvation, you will never know genuine peace and fulfillment.

Repentance is a wonderful thing! Suppose we could sin but were unable to repent. Suppose God let us fall but would not lift us up. Suppose we were able to wander far away but were not able to return. If that were true there would be no hope. There could be no freedom from the slavery of sin.

Yes, my friend, it is the message of repentance that makes the gospel a message of joy. Because of repentance, the sinner can be cleansed; the fallen can be lifted; the prodigal can come home; the enslaved can be freed. You can be changed!

The call to repentance is the major theme throughout the New Testament. The message that John the Baptist preached could be summed up in one word: *repent.* He challenged people to face their sin and turn from it. In Matthew 3:7-8 John told the pious, self-righteous Pharisees, "O generation of vipers, who hath warned you to flee from the wrath to come? Bring forth therefore fruits meet for repentance."

It took tremendous courage for John to preach that message. I have found that most people do not like to be told that they are sinners. Many do not want to repent. This has become the day of the placid pulpit and the comfortable pew. Very few are talking about repentance. It is not an easy message. John the Baptist was beheaded by a king's executioner for preaching the message!

Repentance itself is a widely misunderstood concept. I have found that a great many people have a false idea of what repentance is. I would like to look at three kinds of repentance and see what the Scriptures teach about this most important of subjects.

FALSE REPENTANCE

The first kind of repentance is not really repentance at all, but a kind of false repentance. In fact, there are many false substitutes that people have for repentance.

Repentance is not conviction, although conviction is necessary. It is the ministry of the Holy Spirit to convict us of our sin, true righteousness, and impending judgment. But a man may be convicted and not repent. Conviction is simply the Holy Spirit's revealing a need to the heart. It can lead to genuine repentance, but it is not repentance.

Repentance is not religion. You may be a very religious person and never repent of your sins. The Pharisees were like that, and John the Baptist told them frankly that he doubted their repentance was the real thing.

In Acts 8 we find the interesting story of a man named Simon. Simon heard Philip the evangelist preach and saw him perform miracles. He asked Peter if he, too, could have the gift of performing miracles, and he even offered him money to buy it!

Peter's answer to Simon was, "Thy money perish with thee, because thou hast thought that the gift of God may be purchased with money. Thou hast neither part nor lot in this matter: for thy heart is not right in the sight of God. Repent therefore of this thy wickedness" (vv. 20-22).

Simon was a religious man, outwardly. Simon had been a sorcerer, and according to verses 9-11, he was respected by all the people as a great man of God because of the sorcery he was able to do. Verse 13 tells us that he had believed. But he had believed without repenting. His faith was all in his head, and not in his heart.

Simon's request to Peter revealed that he had never genuinely repented. His was a false repentance. He still desired power, and the admiration of the people. He was religious, and he was personally acquainted with at least three of the apostles. But religion is not repentance, and Simon was not saved.

Repentance is not an intellectual assent to the gospel. Simon believed, but only intellectually. And it is not enough just to believe the facts of the gospel. The kind of faith Simon had did nothing to change him on the inside.

Intellectual faith is good too, but it is not enough. James wrote, "Thou believest that there is one God; thou doest well: the devils also believe, and tremble" (James 2:19). Demons have no choice but to believe the facts about God, but theirs is by no means saving faith. James taught the powerful truth that saving faith always makes a visible difference in a person's life.

Repentance is not simply being sorry for one's sins. To be sorry is not sufficient. Paul wrote to the Corinthians about two kinds of sorrow. "Now I rejoice, not that ye were made sorry, but that ye sorrowed to repentance. . . . For godly sorrow worketh repentance to salvation not to be repented of: but the sorrow of the world worketh death" (2 Corinthians 7:9-10).

Godly sorrow can *lead* to repentance, but it is not the same thing as repentance. And the sorrow of this world leads not to repentance but to death. Why? Because we can mistake it for repentance.

Probably the best example in the Bible of false repentance is that of Judas. Matthew 27 records his repentance for us. "Then Judas, which had betrayed him, when he saw that he was condemned, repented himself, and brought again the thirty pieces of silver to the chief priests and elders, saying, I have sinned in that I have betrayed the innocent blood. . . . And he cast down the pieces of silver in the temple, and departed, and went and hanged himself" (vv. 3-5).

Judas was *convicted*. He realized his sin and saw that he was condemned.

He was *religious*. He had been with the Lord Jesus and the other disciples for three years, and yet he had done nothing to make the other disciples suspect that he was the one that would betray the Lord. He must have even been involved in some of the healings and casting out of demons that all the disciples did.

He was *intellectually persuaded*. He realized that he had betrayed innocent blood. He had seen the Lord's miracles and heard His teaching for those three years. He surely must have believed in his head that Jesus was whom He claimed to be.

And Judas was *sorry*. But his sorrow was the worldly sorrow that leads to death. He was more sorry about his condemnation than about his sin, and so he hanged himself. His was a false repentance.

My friend, conviction, religion, intellectual faith, and sorrow for sin are all good, but even combined they do not equal true repentance. If you have looked to any or all of those things as repentance, then your repentance has been false.

What, then, *is* repentance? If it is not sorrow or conviction or religion or intellectual assent, *what is it?*

Repentance is simply a change. The word itself means "a change of mind," and that is indeed what repentance is, but it goes even deeper than that. It is a change of direction in the mind and heart and life. It is turning *from* sin and self and Satan. And it is turning *to* God.

The Lord Jesus gave an excellent picture of genuine repentance in Luke 18:10-14:

> Two men went up into the temple to pray; the one a Pharisee, and the other a publican. The Pharisee stood and prayed thus with himself, God, I thank thee, that I am not as other men are, extortioners, unjust, adulterers, or even as this publican. I fast twice in the week, I give tithes of all that I possess. And the publican, standing afar off, would not lift up so much as his eyes unto heaven, but smote upon his breast, saying, God be merciful to me a sinner. I tell you, this man went down to his house justified rather than the other: for everyone that exalteth himself shall be abased; and he that humbleth himself shall be exalted.

The outstanding thing about the prayer of the publican is its total selflessness. He wouldn't even lift up his eyes to heaven. He was turning from self and from his sin, and turning to God in absolute repentance.

It is interesting to note the words the Lord Jesus used in connection with the prayer of the Pharisee. He "prayed . . . with himself," says Jesus (v. 11). That is strikingly similar to the words Matthew used about Judas's repentance. "Repented himself" is the terminology in Matthew 27:3.

Neither Judas nor the proud Pharisee had turned from self. They were preoccupied with themselves, looking within—not looking to the Lord. They had not repented, because they had never turned from their thoughts of their own works.

Genuine repentance requires us to turn away from any works of righteousness we might think we have done. It includes a confession of deep need, a rejection of the past, and a whole new direction in life. Without that kind of repentance no one can be saved.

John Wesley taught Greek at Oxford University at the age of twenty-one. He hazarded his life for the gospel in crossing the Atlantic Ocean many times as a missionary. And yet, by his own testimony, he did not know Jesus Christ as his personal Savior until he had a life-changing encounter with the Lord at Aldersgate at the age of thirty-eight. It was then for the first time that he genuinely repented of his sin and experienced the peace and joy of God's cleansing and forgiveness.

Perhaps you have attended church for many years—perhaps, like Wesley, you have been in Christian work for years—but you realize that you never have genuinely repented. You need to turn humbly to the Lord today, my friend, and genuinely repent.

Without repentance, all your religion, all your good works, all your sorrow for your sin, all your resolves to do better—all those things you may have substituted for real repentance—are of no value whatsoever. The Lord Jesus says that unless you repent you will perish.

But, you may be thinking, I thought all that was necessary for salvation was faith. Doesn't the Bible teach that "whosoever believeth in him should not perish, but have everlasting life" (John 3:16)? Yes, that is true. But real faith is not possible without repentance. A person cannot turn to God in faith until he has turned from his sin and self.

SHALLOW REPENTANCE

Let me warn you against a third kind of repentance—shallow repentance. In Revelation 3, the apostle John records a message from the Lord Jesus to the church at

Laodicea. It was a lukewarm church. It was "neither cold nor hot" (v. 16). It had tried to stay away from extremes, and it was a church in real need but unaware of its needs. It was wretched, miserable, poor, blind, and naked.

Verse 19 records the Lord's admonition to that church: "Be zealous therefore, and repent." The Lord was warning the Laodiceans against the dangers of a shallow repentance. He was saying, "Open your eyes, be aware of your needs, repent with zeal. Repent deeply."

Perhaps you are a believer who has grown cold or lukewarm. Perhaps you repented once, but your repentance has become shallow, and you have lost sight of the poverty of your own soul. Will you open your eyes to your needs, and repent?

Repentance is not a one-time act. The attitude of the repentant publican is the attitude every believer should maintain. We are never to be proud or self-righteous. Our repentance should be a deep, constant, ongoing attitude of humble repentance before the Lord.

The Lord can fill only empty vessels. It is not until we are repentant that He can fill us with His power. It is not until we are emptied of self that we can be filled with the Spirit.

Will you repent today, and repent deeply? The Lord is speaking. His message is, "Be zealous, and repent."

8

The Conversion of Cornelius

A crisis can mean life or death! Each day we are confronted by crucial situations. Almost none of us has escaped the effects of one kind of crisis or another.

The conversion of Cornelius was one of those crisis situations. It literally revolutionized the first-century church. It brought life and power to the Great Commission.

In fact, the conversion of Cornelius was a crisis in more than one way. I would like to suggest three ways in which Cornelius's conversion was a crisis.

IT WAS A CRISIS IN GOD'S DEALINGS WITH THE WORLD

First, the conversion of Cornelius was a crisis in God's dealings with the world. Before the Lord Jesus left this earth, He marked out His strategy for carrying the gospel to the whole world. In Acts 1:8, He told His apostles, "But ye shall receive power, after that the Holy Ghost is come upon you: and ye shall be witnesses unto me both in Jerusalem, and in all Judaea, and in Samaria, and unto the uttermost part of the earth."

In Jerusalem the apostles experienced overwhelming success. Thousands were won to Jesus Christ at Pentecost alone.

People were added to the church daily. The church experienced great growth—so much that they could not provide for the physical needs of all the believers.

Things looked good from the outside. But the new Christians were failing to follow *God's* plan. They were cozy and comfortable. There was such great success in Jerusalem. Why should they move on?

Then God allowed great persecution to scatter the Christians to Judea, Samaria, and beyond. The scope of the church broadened to a wider geographic region. But the church's vision needed to be enlarged to see beyond limited ethnic boundaries as well. And the single crisis event that was mostly responsible for that was the conversion of a Gentile military officer by the name of Cornelius.

Today we tend to think of the church as a largely non-Jewish body. But in the beginning it was not that way at all. The earliest church was composed completely of Jews and some Gentiles who had converted to Judaism. The early church was distinctly Hebrew in its beginnings. The Lord Jesus had been born and lived on this earth as a Jew. The apostles were all Jewish. Christ's ministry had for the most part been among the Jewish people. The only Scriptures available to the early church were the Hebrew Old Testament writings.

It was difficult for those in the early church to conceive that God would work in any way other than through the Jews. All God's dealings in the past had been with the nation of Israel. Gentiles were considered dogs, barbarians, unclean. No one expected God to deal directly with them.

That is why the salvation of Cornelius rocked the church to its very center. It was a magnificent declaration of inclusion—a transformation of the church's vision and mission. It was a new beginning in God's dealings with the world.

Everyone was shocked by it! Those that were with Peter

were astonished, we are told in Acts 10:45. Acts 11:2-3 tells us that when Peter returned to Jerusalem, Jewish believers there "contended with him, saying, Thou wentest in to men uncircumcised, and didst eat with them." That was something no self-respecting Jew would do!

But Peter explained to them what had happened, and he concluded his explanation with these words: "What was I, that I could withstand God?" (Acts 11:17). Peter said, "It wasn't my idea, it was God's! There was nothing I could do to stop Him!" God had begun something new. From now on He would deal directly with Gentile and Jew alike. Ethnic and racial distinctions did not matter, for "God is no respecter of persons" (Acts 10:34). The gospel truly would go into all the world, to all men.

Those in the church at Jerusalem recognized that this great crisis signaled a new direction in God's dealings with the world. Their consensus was, "Then hath God also to the Gentiles granted repentance unto life" (Acts 11:18). God was now dealing with Jew and Gentile alike. What a marvelous revelation!

It Was a Crisis in God's Dealings with Peter

The conversion of Cornelius was also a crisis in God's dealings with the apostle Peter. Peter had to be dealt with concerning his prejudice before God could use him completely. In Acts 10:9-10 we are told that "Peter went up upon the housetop to pray about the sixth hour: And he became very hungry, and would have eaten: but while they made ready, he fell into a trance."

Peter saw a vision of a sheet, let down to earth, filled with animals not lawful for any Jewish person to eat. Verse 13 tells us, "There came a voice to him, Rise, Peter; kill, and eat."

Look at Peter's answer in verse 14: "Not so, Lord; for I have never eaten anything that is common or unclean."

Peter recognized the lordship of Christ with his lips, but not with his life! He called Jesus his Lord, but he did not obey Him.

The same thing happened three times, and the sheet was taken back into heaven. Peter pondered the meaning of his vision. "What God hath cleansed, that call not thou common" (v. 15). While he questioned and thought, some men came from Cornelius to call for him. They told him that Cornelius had been instructed by a messenger of God to find Peter and to hear his words.

The next day, Peter went to Cornelius's house. His first words to Cornelius show us that he was learning the lessons God was teaching him. "God hath shewed me that I should not call any man common or unclean" (v. 28).

What was God teaching Peter in this crisis experience? First, He was teaching him about the lordship of Christ. He was asking, "Why call ye me, Lord, Lord, and do not the things which I say?" (Luke 6:46). If Jesus is Lord, we must obey Him implicitly.

Second, He was teaching Peter that he was no longer under the law but under grace. Peter was to have some conflicts with Paul over this same issue later in his ministry. And this experience with Cornelius and the sheet full of animals would be a reminder to him that he was indeed no longer under law but under grace.

Third, God was teaching Peter that He is not prejudiced. Acceptance with God is not based on race, color, national origin, looks, intelligence, or ethnic background. It is not obtained by a religious ceremony, such as circumcision. God deals with each man as an individual.

It Was a Crisis in God's Dealings with Cornelius

Cornelius's conversion was, of course, a crisis in the life of Cornelius as well. Let us consider for a few minutes this man Cornelius. Who was he? What do we know about him?

First of all, he was a soldier. In Acts 10:1, Luke describes him as "a centurion of the band called the Italian band." As a centurion, he commanded a division of one hundred men. He was living in Caesarea, the civil and military capital of the Judean region. He was a part of the Roman police force, and it was his job to keep order.

That was one strike against him. The Jews resented the Roman presence in their land, and Roman soldiers symbolized everything the Jews detested.

In addition, Cornelius was a Gentile. That was another strike against him. The Jews considered him to be outside of the fold of God. It was bad enough that he was living in their land, but the fact that he exercised authority over them was a source of incomprehensible irritation to the Jews.

Cornelius did not seem to be the best candidate to become a partaker of the grace of God.

But God had been working in Cornelius's heart. Acts 10:2 states that he was "a devout man, and one that feared God." He was reverent and faithful in prayer. He was most likely what was referred to as *a Jewish proselyte of the gate.* He had forsaken the paganism of his upbringing and outgrown the superstitions of idolatry. He had perhaps had some exposure to the Greek translation of the Old Testament Scriptures.

He had probably embraced the great principles and writings of Moses and the prophets, but he had not yet actually embraced Judaism. The Jews still considered him unclean, a heathen. But God was working in his heart, and Cornelius was responding.

Acts 10:30-33 is Cornelius's account to Peter of what had happened in this great crisis in his life:

> And Cornelius said, Four days ago I was fasting until this hour; and at the ninth hour I prayed in my house, and, behold, a man stood before me in bright clothing, And said, Cornelius, thy prayer is heard, and thine alms are had

in remembrance in the sight of God. Send therefore to Joppa, and call hither Simon, whose surname is Peter; he is lodged in the house of one Simon a tanner by the sea side: who, when he cometh, shall speak unto thee. Immediately therefore I sent to thee; and thou hast well done that thou art come. Now therefore are we all here present before God, to hear all things that are commanded thee of God.

The message that Peter then gave to Cornelius was the gospel of Jesus Christ, summed up in his concluding words in verse 43, "To him [Christ] give all the prophets witness, that through his name whosoever believeth in him shall receive remission of sins."

Cornelius did believe, and God poured out His Holy Spirit on him, and on those who came with him and believed as well. God had shared His Son, His salvation, and His Spirit with the Gentiles!

Cornelius's life was transformed. Up to this point, he had been interested in spiritual things, but now he had the Spirit of God living in him! Cornelius had offered prayer, but now he knew God in a personal way! He had given his money, but now God had given him life!

Look at all Cornelius received in this great crisis experience. He received *remission of his sins.* That is what Peter had promised in the name of Christ to those who would believe. Cornelius had fasted and prayed, given alms, and sought to know God. But he had never known the peace of having his sins forgiven.

He received *the Holy Spirit.* The presence of the Spirit of God was evident in the same way as on the day of Pentecost. Cornelius and those with him spoke in unlearned foreign languages. That was proof that the Holy Spirit had come to the Gentiles in exactly the same sense as to the Jews.

He received *eternal life.* The whole impact of this account is that Cornelius, a Gentile, was saved. He was accepted into God's family, released from the power of sin and death.

What a wonderful crisis experience! All at once, God was dealing with Cornelius, with Peter, and with the whole world. He was building His church. And everyone had some wonderful truth to learn from it.

What can you learn from it?

Perhaps you, like Peter, need to be purged of prejudices. Prejudice is an ugly thing. It is a crushing sin, controlling the hearts of men and affecting their attitudes and conduct. But there is no prejudice or respect of persons with God.

The word *prejudice* means "pre-judging." It is opinion without evidence. It is determination without investigation, condemnation without trial. It is forming an opinion without due knowledge of the facts. It is giving unreasonable bent to one side of a cause or issue. Prejudice is absolutely contrary to the character of God.

If there is prejudice or class hatred in your life, you need to seek God's forgiveness and cleansing.

Or perhaps you are like Peter in that you need to learn the truth of absolute submission to the lordship of Jesus Christ in your life. Maybe you have been calling Him Lord at the same time that you have been refusing and denying Him. Submit to Him now.

Or maybe you are like Cornelius—religious, but lost. Apart from faith in Jesus Christ, Cornelius would have perished; the same is true of you.

From the story of Cornelius's conversion we learn that *salvation is available to all men.* Let us not lose sight of the accompanying truth that *all men need to be saved.* Cornelius's religion did not make him acceptable in the sight of God. He needed to repent, to trust Christ, and to be saved. That is true of every man. Each of us must experience the crisis of salvation in our lives.

And salvation *is* a crisis experience. You cannot *grow* into the Christian faith. You cannot *back* into Christianity. You cannot *slide* into salvation. Everyone who is saved passed from death unto life at a definite point in his life.

Have you experienced such a crisis? Is there a definite time in your life that you can point to and say, "That was when I passed from death unto life"? Perhaps you cannot point to the exact minute, hour, or even day, but do you know that there was a definite time and place when you were saved?

The gospel of Christ is the great leveler of society. Everyone stands equal at the foot of the cross. God's salvation belongs to all who will repent and believe. No matter who you are, no matter what your place in life, Christ will receive you if you will come to Him right now.

9

A Personal Revolution

For years, psychologists have been saying that it is impossible to change a person. They say that you can rearrange an individual's environment, you can adjust his ambition and goals, you can give him an education, but you can never *really* change him.

Humanly speaking that theory may be very sound, but in the spiritual realm it is absolutely false. Millions of people in this world can testify—along with me—that a man, woman, boy, or girl *can* be radically transformed in life or action through a personal relationship with the Lord Jesus Christ.

The apostle Paul wrote, "Therefore if any man be in Christ, he is a new creature: old things are passed away; behold, all things are become new" (2 Corinthians 5:17). That is a promise from the Word of God! We can be totally changed—become new creatures.

No one was more qualified to pen that verse of Scripture than the apostle Paul. His life was a classic example of a life totally transformed by the changing power of Jesus Christ. If ever a man was stopped right in his tracks and magnificently changed in every way, Paul was that man.

Let's look into Paul's life and examine three marvelous changes the Lord wrought in him.

HIS PURPOSE WAS CHANGED

First, Paul's purpose was dramatically changed. The book of Acts relates that Saul of Tarsus was actively engaged in a deliberate program to eradicate Christianity. He hated it and everything it stood for.

The first time we are introduced to this man is in Acts 7—at the martyrdom of Stephen. Verse 58 tells us that the witnesses—probably the people who stoned him—laid their clothes at the feet of Saul, who was consenting unto Stephen's death. Saul stood by and watched the brutal stoning of Stephen and even guarded the coats of those who threw the stones.

By the next chapter, Saul became more aggressive. Acts 8:3 says that Saul "made havock of the church, entering into every house, and haling men and women committed them to prison." He became the chief persecutor of the early church.

Like many of the Jewish religious leaders of the first century, Saul was enraged by the claims of the new Christians that Jesus was Israel's Messiah. That this man Jesus could be considered divine was to Saul nothing less than blasphemy, and his anger increased his zeal and fervor in persecuting believers in this new sect.

But one day his whole being was shaken. God took hold of him and said, "It's time for a change." Out on a highway leading to Damascus, Saul was arrested by the Lord Himself. While traveling along the road, Saul was suddenly blinded by a light that surrounded him.

> And he fell to the earth, and heard a voice saying unto him, Saul, Saul, why persecutest thou me? And he said, Who art thou, Lord? And the Lord said, I am Jesus whom thou persecutest [Acts 9:4-5a].

Saul had started on the road to Damascus to find Christians there to persecute, but he was stopped short by the Lord Himself, and his whole life purpose began to undergo a total change. He undoubtedly felt he was doing the right thing in his attempt to stamp out Christianity, but he found that he was really fighting God!

This encounter represented a crisis in the life of Saul, who subsequently came to be known as Paul. For when he cried out, "Who art thou, Lord?" he was acknowledging the lordship of Jesus Christ! The same man who had been casting men and women into prison for their faith in Jesus Christ had just acknowledged Jesus' lordship. Saul called Jesus *Lord!*

Yes, Saul's conversion *was* sudden. The Scriptures contain examples of others who came to Christ after long periods of time, but Saul's conversion was a definite, dramatic experience of immediate change. Saul, the chief persecutor of the church, was about to become Paul, its chief missionary! Saul, the murderer, would become Paul, the martyr! Scarcely a man in the history of the world has undergone a more dramatic change of purpose than Saul of Tarsus. His zeal was the same as ever. His intensity had not diminished. His dedication was, if anything, more sure than before, only now it was aimed in the opposite direction. The very thing he once opposed now became his life's work. All that he had stood for in the past he now fought. What a dramatic, powerful change!

Just read through the book of Acts to see the effects of Paul's ministry. Wherever he went he started a new church. He won people to faith in Jesus Christ. He preached. He was persecuted, stoned, and even left for dead because of his testimony for Jesus Christ.

Yes, my friend, Saul had a new purpose in life. But that was not all that changed.

Saul had a new perspective. He saw things differently from that moment on. A flash of light had blinded his eyes. He could not see at all for some time, and I believe that was God's way of showing Saul that he had always been blind— spiritually blind. That flash of light may have blinded Saul's physical eyes, but it opened his spiritual eyes.

Consider for a moment the background of this man. Saul was a Jew born in Asia Minor, in the city of Tarsus. He had received the finest education possible in his day under the tutelege of the famous scholar Gamaliel. He was a Pharisee, belonging to the strictest Jewish sect, holding rigidly to the law of Moses.

He had probably been named after Saul, the first king of Israel. The name means "Big One." King Saul had been physically large—he stood head and shoulders above all other men. Saul of Tarsus was large in ambition and intellect. He had virtually every advantage of his day.

In his letter to believers at Philippi, Paul lists his credentials and heritage. He says that he was "circumcised the eighth day, of the stock of Israel, of the tribe of Benjamin, an Hebrew of the Hebrews; as touching the law, a Pharisee . . . touching the righteousness which is in the law, blameless" (Philippians 3:5-6).

Do you see Paul's perspective before he was saved? He looked at things from a human perspective. Comparing himself with other men was a source of pride to him. He was like the Pharisee the Lord Jesus spoke of in Luke 18:11-12, who stood in the Temple and prayed, "God, I thank thee, that I am not as other men are, extortioners, unjust, adulterers, or even as this publican. I fast twice in the week, I give tithes of all that I possess."

From a human perspective, Saul of Tarsus had much to be proud of. His education, his heritage, his family, his knowledge of the law and strict adherence to it, were all the kinds of things other men looked up to him for.

But there was one thing that Saul, like that Pharisee in the Temple, could not see—his own sin. With all the spiritual and material benefits Saul had, he could not see his need for salvation!

But the Lord Jesus changed that. The apostle Paul gained a deep awareness of his sin and weakness.

And God gave Paul a special reminder. Paul called it "a thorn in the flesh, the messenger of Satan to buffet me, lest I should be exalted above measure" (2 Corinthians 12:7). We do not know exactly what it was, but it was some kind of infirmity that kept Paul perpetually aware of his weakness.

Paul asked the Lord three times to remove that thorn in the flesh, but the Lord's answer to him was, "My grace is sufficient for thee: for my strength is made perfect in weakness" (2 Corinthians 12:9). As a result, Paul said that he would most gladly glory in his infirmities. His perspective had been changed. Before, he had looked at himself and seen his strength, but now he saw his sin. Before, he had looked at himself and seen wisdom, but now he saw weakness.

In 1 Corinthians 15:9 Paul wrote to the church at Corinth, "For I am the least of the apostles, that am not meet to be called an apostle, because I persecuted the church of God."

Several years later, he wrote to the Ephesians, "Unto me, who am less than the least of all saints, is this grace given" (Ephesians 3:8).

Then near the end of his life, he wrote to Timothy, "Christ Jesus came into the world to save sinners; of whom I am chief" (1 Timothy 1:15).

Do you see how Paul's humility developed as his awareness of his own sin grew? He began as a proud Pharisee, denying any need. Arrested by the Lord and confronted with his own sin, he was given the office of apostle. But he saw himself as the least of the apostles. Then he saw himself as less than the least of saints. Then he saw himself as the chief of sinners. What a wonderful change of perspective!

HIS PERSONALITY WAS CHANGED

His purpose had been changed. His perspective had been changed. And there was a third change in Paul. His personality was changed.

Consider Saul's personality before his dramatic encounter with the Lord Jesus on the road to Damascus. By nature, he was obviously an intense man. He was a man of almost fanatical convictions. Those things were true of him even after his conversion. Even so, there was a noticeable difference between the personality of Saul of Tarsus and the personality of Paul the apostle.

Saul was virtually a psychopath. His intense convictions and almost fanatical zeal made him violent. He was a persecutor. He was cruel. He was vicious.

Can you imagine the scene at the stoning of Stephen? Stephen had preached his heart out. He had said some challenging things, and he obviously knew the Scriptures well. When he was being brutally stoned, he prayed for forgiveness for his persecutors. His face shone with a sense of the peace of God. As he was dying, he showed only peace, no fear. He was confident. He was fully surrendered to the Lord Jesus.

Only the coldest kind of person could stand by and watch Stephen die and not be touched by his faith and gentleness and the confident, compassionate way in which he died. But Saul stood there unmoved. In fact, if Stephen's death did anything to Saul of Tarsus, it made him more determined than ever to persecute Christians. What kind of man must he have been?

But when Saul of Tarsus encountered the Lord Jesus, all that changed. His first words to the Lord were, "Lord, what wilt thou have me to do?" (Acts 9:6). And those words characterized the rest of Paul's life.

Instead of a proud, arrogant Pharisee, ruthless and cruel in persecuting the church, Paul became a humble, submissive apostle, and he himself was persecuted.

Do you see what a transformation there was in Paul's life? He changed from hating the Lord and everything He stood for to acknowledging Him as Lord in his own life and giving his life in service. Paul went anywhere and everywhere for the Lord Jesus.

Let me suggest several truths in the account of Paul's conversion that none of us can afford to miss.

First, the more a man allows God to change him, the more useful that man is to the Lord. The secret to Paul's effectiveness as an apostle was his total surrender to the transforming power of Christ. There was no area of Paul's life that was closed to God. There was nothing in Paul's life that was off limits to the Holy Spirit.

My friend, God uses us to the degree that we commit ourselves to Him. He can best use you if you surrender to Him unconditionally.

A second truth we see from the conversion of Paul is that the Lord can save anyone. It seemed that of all the people in Judea in the first century, Saul of Tarsus was the least likely to accept Christ as Savior. But the Lord worked a miracle in his life. There is no one who cannot be reached by the saving power of the Lord Jesus. God can transform the life of anyone who will turn to him.

Finally, if Saul of Tarsus needed salvation, so do you and I. Saul was a student and teacher of the Scriptures. He was a strict follower of the law. He had dedicated his life to his religion. But he was not saved.

My friend, have you experienced a change in your life? Have you allowed the Lord Jesus to come in and revolutionize your life? Have You trusted Him and received eternal life?

In my ministry I have met many kinds of people in the same kind of situation as Saul of Tarsus—religious, but lost. I've talked with Sunday school teachers, deacons, choir members, and (believe it or not) even ministers of churches who have come to confess that in spite of many years of religious service they've never really had this personal confrontation with Jesus Christ. Unfortunately there are many who profess salvation but do not possess salvation.

How about you ? Could your life use a change? Why not surrender to the Lord Jesus right now? Trust Him for salvation. He will give you eternal life and transform you as He did Saul of Tarsus.

10

The Mystery of Imparted Life

It could have been your life or mine. But it happened, instead, to an asbestos worker in Pittsburgh, Pennsylvania. His name was Robert McFall.

McFall became sick and was given only months to live. The problem was his blood. Due to a deficiency in his bone marrow, doctors said, his body could not produce the red blood cells and platelets essential to his life. The only thing that could save his life was a bone marrow transplant from a related person.

After some tests, doctors determined that the only potential donor was a cousin, David Shimp, but he held back. The transplant process, a painful procedure, was forbidding. Shimp felt that the hazards were too great.

The sick man sued. Understandably, he was desperate for a transplant, and he thought he could compel his cousin to be a donor. But the court denied his plea. Said the judge, "In our law, there's no duty to save someone else's life."

The story has a sad ending. Robert McFall died, and David Shimp was left to wonder if he had made the right decision.

"I feel terrible," he said. "But he asked me for something I couldn't give."

Our hearts go out to both men—the one who died, and the one who was asked to make such a difficult decision. But their experience, by way of contrast, shows the wonder of the greatest act of compassion of all history, the death of Christ.

The wonderful truth that makes the death of the Lord Jesus so meaningful is the fact that His death was a voluntary offering of His blood for your sake and for mine.

His blood? Yes, that is what the apostle John, in Revelation 1:5, wrote about. "Unto him that loved us, and washed us from our sins in his own blood." John was saying that it is blood that saves men and women from their sins—the lifeblood of a Person who was Himself sinless. And the Bible teaches that it is blood, and only blood, that can atone for sin (see Leviticus 17:11). No wonder the Bible has so much to say about the blood of Christ.

But many today find references to the blood of Christ offensive. John Stott, a British clergyman, tells of an angry letter from a lady who had visited his church in London. She objected to a hymn sung in the service that spoke of the blood of Jesus Christ.

And she is not alone. There are many worldwide to whom any mention of the blood of Christ is offensive. Some denominations have removed from their hymnbooks hymns that mention the blood of Christ. The remedy, however, is not to set aside such hymns, but to understand them. In his reply to the woman, Dr. Stott pointed out that such references are "symbols to be understood, rather than pictures to be imagined." Wise advice. The meaning of the blood of Jesus Christ is crucial to the Christian faith. Throw it out, and you have cast away the heart of the atonement.

We must remember that it is God Himself in His Word who directs our attention to the blood of Christ. And His emphasis on the blood has a purpose. We do well to grasp it.

What is God saying when he speaks of blood? The key to

understanding lies in the Old Testament in Leviticus 17:11: "For the life of the flesh is in the blood: and I have given it to you upon the altar to make an atonement for your souls: for it is the blood that maketh an atonement for the soul."

What an amazing revelation! Fourteen hundred years before Christ, our great Creator told Moses that physical life is closely linked with blood. It took medical science some three thousand years to make that same discovery. For centuries, blood was one of four bodily fluids doctors linked with life. That view continued through the middle ages.

The discovery that blood circulates through the body was made in 1628 by the English physician William Harvey. Even after that, the practice of draining blood from sick people was continued for more than a century. It was thought that bleeding hastened healing by allowing poison to escape the system. We now know that the opposite is true.

Today our understanding of the value of blood has led to blood banks and transfusions. Most of our modern techniques for saving life with blood have originated since World War II.

Yes, the life of the flesh is in the blood, and today a junior high school student could tell you why. Our bodies are made of cells. Each one is dependent upon oxygen brought by the blood for life. Each cell is dependent upon the blood for nourishment and waste removal, and there are probably a quadrillion cells in your body.

My friend, your blood is a miracle fluid, made up of living cells, as many as five and a half million cells in a cubic centimeter of blood. And your body is constantly manufacturing cells to make up for those that die, at the rate of two million per second!

Yes, blood is life, a miracle from God. It is a gift that could have been created only by an all-wise Being.

Small wonder, then, that God commands great respect for

blood. Genesis 9:5 warns that God himself will hold both man and beast responsible for the shedding of human blood.

Think for a moment about what a wonderful thing it is that the Lord Jesus Christ would offer His own blood for sinful man. Here are three wonderful truths about the blood of Jesus Christ.

JESUS' BLOOD IS EXPENSIVE

First, the blood of Jesus Christ is costly. The price of forgiveness of sins is a price no one but the sinless Son of God could pay. Its value is beyond human understanding.

How often we try to rationalize our sins by saying, "I can make up for this by doing better next time." Not so, my friend, when we have sinned. Nothing we can say or do will wipe a single sin off God's eternal record.

Sin must be paid for, and the price is blood. And it must be the blood of One who had no sin—the blood of Jesus Christ. How can its value be calculated? He had to come as a man, suffer the shame and agony of the cross, and give His very life.

If you want to get a sense of the depth of Christ's sufferings, study Isaiah 53, Psalm 22, or Psalm 69. All of those passages were prophetic, indicating that He knew when he came exactly what He would suffer, and yet He did it anyway. What a tremendous price to pay!

Or watch as Jesus prays in agony in the garden of Gethsemane. Three times He prayed, "O my Father, if it be possible, let this cup pass from me: nevertheless not as I will, but as thou wilt" (Matthew 26:39). Luke 22:44 tells us that "his sweat was as it were great drops of blood falling down to the ground."

Read the account of His crucifixion in the four gospels. He was spat upon. He was brutally whipped with a Roman scourge, a vicious whip made of many long strands of leather with little pieces of metal and bone attached to the ends to tear the victim's flesh. He had a cruel crown of long, sharp thorns thrust onto His head. He was ridiculed, stripped, beaten, and mocked. He had nails driven through His hands and feet. A sword pierced His side. It was a slow, agonizing, painful way to die. But He was shedding His blood for you and for me; His blood was costly.

JESUS' BLOOD IS EFFECTUAL

The second great truth about Jesus' blood is that it is effectual. That means that it does what it was intended to do. The greatest power the world will ever know is the power released by the blood of Jesus Christ. That blood gave lost men a whole new standing before God. It restored relations with God. It opened a whole new way of blessing.

You see, the Lord Jesus' death had no atoning value apart from the blood, because God's way of sacrifice has always been by the shedding of blood. Hebrews 9:22 says, "Without shedding of blood is no remission."

And the purpose for which the Lord Jesus shed His blood was for the remission of sins. He said so before His death. "This is my blood of the new testament, which is shed for many" (Mark 14:24), He said, as He passed the cup at the Last Supper.

The apostle Paul taught that justification was possible only through Jesus' blood. In Romans 5:9 he said, "Much more then, being now justified by his blood, we shall be saved from wrath through him."

The blood of Christ wipes out the certainty of judgment. It assures men of God's favor and gives us access to the throne of grace. It enables us to live a whole new kind of life. It assures us of forgiveness and eternity in heaven. It purges our conscience. It cleanses our sins. It seals the new covenant with God.

In the Old Testament, blood offerings were required. Most Bible students believe that the reason Cain's sacrifice was rejected by God while Abel's was accepted is that Cain's sacrifice was a bloodless sacrifice of the fruit of the ground. Abel, on the other hand had sacrificed one of the firstlings of the flock. Hebrews 11:4 says that "Abel offered a more excellent sacrifice than Cain."

The blood was necessary to make atonement. *Atonement* means "a covering," and Hebrews 10:4 says, "It is not possible that the blood of bulls and goats should take away sins." Those sacrifices were symbolic, a covering for sins that were not taken away. And the blood of those sacrifices illustrated the blood of a perfect sacrifice, one that would be offered only once, and one that would not just be a covering for sins. The perfect sacrifice would remove sins forever.

Hebrews 10:11-12 says, "And every high priest standeth daily ministering and offering oftentimes the same sacrifices, which can never take away sins: But this man, after he had offered one sacrifice for sins for ever, sat down on the right hand of God."

Jesus' blood is effectual. It does what it was intended to do: it removes sin and the effects of sin forever, as the blood of an animal sacrifice could not. The high priest was kept so busy offering the same sacrifices over and over that he never had time to sit down on the job! The Temple had all kinds of furniture, but no chairs!

But the Lord Jesus offered His blood as the perfect sacrifice. It was offered only once, forever, and then He sat down at God's right hand. His blood is effectual.

JESUS' BLOOD IS ESSENTIAL

A third great truth about the blood of Jesus Christ is that it is absolutely essential. Do you see the fallacy of removing the great hymns that refer to the blood of Jesus from our hymnbooks? Without the shed blood of Jesus Christ, we would have no need for a hymnbook at all. Our lives would be futile. We would have no hope.

Yes, my friend, the blood of Jesus Christ is essential. Jesus taught this great truth long before that crisis week with His disciples in Jerusalem. "I am the living bread," He said in John 6:51. "If any man eat of this bread, he shall live forever: and the bread that I will give is my flesh, which I will give for the life of the world."

We know what Jesus was saying. Looking ahead to the shadows of the crucifixion, He was saying, "I am giving myself as a sacrifice. I am going to die for your sins, and you must by faith partake of Me as your sacrifice." But it was a difficult thing, understandably, for those who heard Him then to grasp.

He went on further to speak particularly of His blood.

> Verily, verily, I say unto you, Except ye eat the flesh of the Son of man, and drink his blood, ye have no life in you. Whoso eateth my flesh, and drinketh my blood, hath eternal life; and I will raise him up at the last day. For my flesh is meat indeed, and my blood is drink indeed. . . . he that eateth me, even he shall live by me [John 6:53-55, 57b].

Our Lord never spoke words more difficult to understand than those. Those words have been misapplied and misinterpreted possibly more than any other words in all the Bible.

And yet the truth that Jesus was teaching was simple. To benefit from a sacrifice, one must partake of it. The Hebrews were instructed to eat the Passover lamb that was sacrificed. The Lord was teaching that we must partake of His sacrifice—not, of course, by literally eating and drinking, but by faith.

He was saying, "I will pay the price. I will make the great sacrifice of my blood, and you can have the benefit. But you must receive it for yourself. You must partake of it by faith."

Remember God's Word through his servant Moses: "The

life of the flesh is in the blood: and I have given it to you upon the altar to make an atonement for your souls" (Leviticus 17:11). There can be no remission of your sins apart from the shedding of the blood of Jesus Christ.

Dr. James M. Gray, for many years a faithful president of Moody Bible Institute, wrote in 1900 what has become a favorite hymn:

> Nor silver nor gold hath obtained my redemption;
> Nor riches of earth could have saved my poor soul.
> The blood of the cross is my only foundation.
> The death of my Savior now maketh me whole.
> I am redeemed, but not with silver,
> I am bought, but not with gold;
> Bought with a price—the blood of Jesus,
> Precious price of love untold.

Those words are based on 1 Peter 1:18-19: "Forasmuch as ye know that ye were not redeemed with corruptible things, as silver and gold . . . but with the precious blood of Christ, as of a lamb without blemish and without spot."

Have you partaken of that great sacrifice? Are you redeemed? Do you know Him? His blood is one great thing you cannot do without.

11

The Brazen Serpent

"You can't teach an old dog new tricks."

That's the way the saying goes. Whether it is true or not is, of course, debatable. But at least it points out a basic flaw in human nature—people do become set in their ways. And more than that, most folks are very predictable.

That was true of the children of Israel. The story of their departure from Egypt and wanderings in the wilderness is the story of rebellion. They had rebelled against Moses. They had rebelled against God. They had murmured and complained. Worst of all, they had longed to be back in Egypt.

SIN

In Numbers 21 we find the Israelites persisting in their old ways. Thirty-eight years had passed since God had led them out of Egypt. They had not been able to enter the Promised Land because of their unbelief, so God had sustained them for all of those years in the wilderness. God had fed them, led them, and delivered them from every crisis that had threatened them. They had seen His works, beheld his glory, and experienced His loving care for them.

Now a new crisis had developed. Some Canaanites, led by King Arad, had ambushed the Israelites and captured some of them.

Israel came running to the Lord with a vow. In verse 2 we read, "And Israel vowed a vow unto the LORD, and said, If thou wilt indeed deliver this people into my hand, then I will utterly destroy their cities."

The following verse tells us that God heard them. Israel was delivered, and, keeping their vow to the Lord, they destroyed the enemy.

But, as so often happened in the history of Israel, and as too often happens in our lives, the great victory was followed by a terrible defeat. The old problems of disobedience and discouragement began to plague the people. Notice verse 4: "And they journeyed from mount Hor by the way of the Red sea, to compass the land of Edom: and the soul of the people was much discouraged because of the way."

They became tired. Watch out that Satan does not take advantage of you when you are tired. They were discouraged, it says, "because of the way." I am sure that there were many in that company who remembered the miraculous deliverance from Egypt. There were a number who had been stirred by God's power in opening the Red Sea. They had seen it with their eyes. They had been there when it happened. They had marched through that sea on dry land, while God held the walls of water on either side of them. They had seen God's great hand of mercy, time and time again, as He provided water in a dry place, rained down manna from heaven, and met their every need.

They had sung a song of redemption. But now they had to go around Edom. That meant a long, hard walk, with many hills and valleys and more burning desert. Their song of redemption turned to a grumble.

Aren't we often like that? You know, it is not really an easy road that we are called to follow. There are valleys and hills and sometimes the burning deserts. It is easy to get discouraged. Amid the problems of Edom, it is easy to forget how bad Egypt was.

Complaining was nothing new to the Israelites. But here we find that their murmuring took a new twist. Before, their complaints had been directly aimed at Aaron and Moses. But now they spoke out blatantly against God. Verse 5 says, "And the people spake against God, and against Moses, Wherefore have ye brought us up out of Egypt to die in the wilderness? for there is no bread, neither is there any water; and our soul loatheth this light bread."

Can you imagine such ingratitude after forty years of miraculous care? God had provided them with manna for every day they had been in the wilderness. It was perfect to supply every need they had, yet they had the audacity to tell God that they hated it. This was the height of ingratitude and rebellion.

SERPENTS

For the people's rebellion, God sent judgment, the unavoidable consequence of sin. "And the LORD sent fiery serpents among the people, and they bit the people; and much people of Israel died" (v. 6).

The Israelites had sinned, failing to honor and obey God. "The wages of sin is death," according to Romans 6:23. So the Israelites were collecting their wages—in the form of poisonous snakes.

My friend, sin must be punished. God, merciful and kind as He is, cannot simply overlook our sin. Someone must pay the price.

It is an unchangeable rule of the universe that "whatsoever a man soweth, that shall he also reap" (Galatians 6:7). God cannot be mocked. And He simply cannot ignore sin. Sin is a direct challenge to His holiness. All sin must be dealt with, and paid for.

But why serpents? We know from the Scriptures as far back as the Garden of Eden and as far into the future as the book of Revelation that the serpent was a symbol of Satan. It seems to me that God was graphically teaching the Israelites that they would reap what they sowed. If they followed Satan and rebelled against God, their judgment would directly relate to their sin. If they followed the serpent, they would be killed by serpents.

Their judgment is a lesson for us, too. Paul refers to this account in his advice to the Christians at Corinth:

> Neither let us tempt Christ, as some of them also tempted, and were destroyed of serpents. Neither murmur ye, as some of them also murmured, and were destroyed of the destroyer. Now all these things happened unto them for ensamples: and they are written for our admonition, upon whom the ends of the world are come [1 Corinthians 10:9-11].

Why were they written for our admonition? Precisely because we are so inclined to fall into the same sins as the Israelites. The sin that they committed is exactly like what we are daily tempted to do. Their severe judgment was meant to be a lesson to us as well.

My friend, do not take sin lightly. When you see it in your life, deal with it. In 1 Corinthians 11:31, the apostle Paul informs the Corinthians, "If we would judge ourselves, we should not be judged."

SALVATION

But the real lesson of the account in Numbers 21 is a lesson of salvation, not of judgment. Look at verses 7-9:

> Therefore the people came to Moses, and said, We have sinned, for we have spoken against the Lord, and against thee; pray unto the LORD, that he take away the serpents from us. And Moses prayed for the people. And the LORD

said unto Moses, Make thee a fiery serpent, and set it upon a pole: and it shall come to pass, that every one that is bitten, when he looketh upon it, shall live. And Moses made a serpent of brass, and put it upon a pole, and it came to pass, that if a serpent had bitten any man, when he beheld the serpent of brass, he lived.

God's instruction to Moses was to construct a serpent of brass and put it up on a pole, so that it would be visible to all. That serpent of brass was a picture of the Lord Jesus Christ, the ultimate cure for sin. When the people who had been bitten by the deadly serpents simply turned their eyes to the uplifted serpent, they would live.

It is interesting to note that the ingredient God was looking for in His people was faith. Faith was necessary there in the wilderness, and it is necessary today for those who look to the cross of Christ for salvation.

All that was required of those people in the wilderness was enough faith to look at the brass serpent on the pole. A simple look of faith would save them.

There were a number of things that they were *not* told to do. For instance, we notice that they were not told to find or prepare a healing medicine. It doesn't take a great deal of imagination to see those afflicted people running here and there looking for some kind of medicinal plant to heal their wounds. I can picture some experimenting with various herbs, some traveling far into the wilderness, not realizing that every step took them away from the real cure for their snakebites: the uplifted serpent of brass.

We also find that they were not told to fight off the serpents. Humanly speaking, that approach might have seemed quite logical. They could have mounted a massive "Kill the Snakes" campaign. But the fact was that this kind of predicament could not be overcome by merely human means. The serpents were a judgment from God. No human plan of attack could eliminate the snakes.

The third thing we discover is that God did not ask the people for any kind of payment. There was nothing for them to do to atone for the sin they had committed. They were not told to offer a sacrifice. They were not told to give money. They were not told to do any good works to make up for their evil. They were simply to look, and they would live.

What a picture of grace! Grace demands nothing, asks for nothing, requires nothing. Grace does not say "do"; it says "done." The minute anything is offered in return for grace, it ceases to be grace. The people were not asked to give, but to receive.

There are several striking parallels between this brazen serpent and the Lord Jesus Christ. Both were "lifted up." The serpent was lifted up on the pole, and the Lord Jesus was lifted up on a cross. Both require only faith for salvation. The Lord Jesus said, "As Moses lifted up the serpent in the wilderness, even so must the Son of man be lifted up: that whosoever believeth in him should not perish, but have eternal life" (John 3:14-15).

The requirement is simply a look of faith! There are no works to do; there is no medicine to obtain; there are no snakes to kill. Simply turn to Him in faith, and you will be saved.

It is astounding how many people I meet who are trying to earn their way to heaven in one way or another. Some think simply attending church is enough to do it. Others try to live by the Ten Commandments or the Sermon on the Mount or the golden rule, thinking that will be enough. Others go through religious rituals. Others give money to various charities.

But do you see the folly of thinking that such acts will earn favor in God's eyes? Such thinking is really a denial and rejection of God's Grace.

Let me illustrate. Suppose an Israelite had been bitten by

one of the fiery serpents. He knew that, left to itself, the snakebite would be fatal. He had seen others deteriorate and die. And he had heard of the brazen serpent. He knew that people had simply looked at it and survived the bites of the serpents. But he thought it was a foolish idea. How could a look at a brass snake save a person?

A friend comes to him. "Why don't you go and look at Moses' brass serpent?" he suggests. "I looked at it, and I lived."

"I don't believe a snake on a pole can do anything for me," the man says. "Besides, if I stand out there and look at it, people will see. They will know I was bitten. Or worse, they might think I am foolish."

"But," says his friend, "this is your only hope! No one has survived the serpent bite except those who have looked at the snake."

The man thinks about it for a while, but he decides to go out and see if he can find some snakebite medicine.

He looks for an hour or so but finds nothing to help him. He feels his strength leaving him. He knows he is dying. He goes back to his tent and lies down.

His friend finds him there. "You must look at the brazen serpent!" he says. "Come outside now, while there is still some time."

"I just don't feel quite ready now," he says. "Wait until I feel better."

"But you will *never* feel better," pleads his friend. "You are getting sicker."

"Perhaps I am too sick for the snake to do me any good," says the man.

"No," says his friend. "Others in worse shape than you have been healed. Come now!"

But the man refuses. He offers a few more excuses—he knows a man who looked at the snake and lived, but that man is a hypocrite. He has too many other things to think about anyway.

The man dies.

What would you think of such a man? He was foolish, wasn't he? And yet there are many people right now who are just like that hypothetical Israelite. They stumble at the simplicity of the gospel. They make excuses. They put it off.

There is no hope for a person who persists like that.

Look and live! This is the call of God. It is the only requirement He makes. And the only way to be saved from our sins is to look to the Lord Jesus Christ in faith. He died on that cross to pay the price of our sins, and He rose again to demonstrate His victory over sin and death and Satan.

He is the only hope in a dying world.

Do not make excuses, my friend. Nothing else matters. What people might think does not matter. How good you are does not matter. What you have done does not matter. You must look to the Lord Jesus Christ and believe and be saved.

12

The Love of God

In 1867, D. L. Moody visited Ireland and met a young teacher-preacher by the name of Harry Moorehouse. Moorehouse was a small, clean-shaven, boyish man with a heavy Lancashire accent. He was a converted pickpocket.

"If I am ever in Chicago, I'll preach for you," offered Moorehouse.

"If you come west, call on me," offered Moody, perhaps not ever really expecting to hear from him again.

But Moorehouse did come, and Moody did let him preach, and his message revolutionized the ministry of D. L. Moody. Night after night, Harry Moorehouse preached on the same familiar and beloved text, John 3:16. Of course you know it, "For God so loved the world, that he gave his only begotten Son, that whosoever believeth in him should not perish, but have everlasting life."

At first, Mr. Moody was openly annoyed at Moorehouse's selection of such a familiar Bible text and his night-after-night exposition of the same theme. He would begin with the text, and then illustrate the love of God from other Scripture accounts. His message was different every night, but the theme and text were always the same.

But something beautiful and life-changing began to happen to Mr. Moody. The truth of God's love began to overwhelm his soul! He saw God from a new perspective. Before, all he had seen was the wrath of God and His hatred for sin. Now he saw as he had never seen before the depth of God's compassion and His love and mercy to sinners. D. L. Moody was never the same again.

In his biography of D. L. Moody, Richard Day gives Moody's own account: "I never knew up to that time that God loved me so much. This heart of mine began to thaw out; I just couldn't keep back the tears. I just drank it all in. I will tell you, there is one thing that draws above everything else, and that is the love of God."

Mr. Moody was so taken with the truth of God's love and moved by it that he had the phrase "God is love" carefully printed on the light globes in the old Moody Church that once stood where the girls' dormitory now stands at Moody Bible Institute.

"I took up that word *Love*," Moody said, "and I do not know how many weeks I spent in studying the passages in which it occurs, till at last I could not help loving people! I had been feeding on love so long that I was anxious to do good to everybody I came in contact with.

"I got full of it. It ran out my fingers. You take up the subject of love in the Bible! You will get so full of it that all you have got to do is to open your lips, and a flood of the love of God flows out."

What a marvelous experience! And yet, I find that even today, most people do not fully understand the love of God.

As a child, I had a dreadful fear of God. I thought of God as a judge sitting upon a great white throne, ready and anxious to pour out vengeance because of my sin. Then I thought that, because Jesus died for me, God *had* to love me.

That's wrong. That's false. Jesus did not die so that God

could love me. God already loved me so much "that He gave His only begotten Son." Every time I read this great verse, John 3:16, three great truths about the love of God come to mind.

THE MYSTERY OF GOD'S LOVE

The first great thing I think about in connection with John 3:16 is the mystery of God's love. Why should God love us? Well, really, I don't know. As I ponder the greatness of God, I wonder why He should love me.

David wondered at the same thing. In Psalm 8 he wrote, "When I consider thy heavens, the work of thy fingers, the moon and the stars, which thou hast ordained; What is man, that thou art mindful of him? and the son of man, that thou visitest him?" (vv. 3-4).

Yes, God is great. In the beginning, He said, "Let there be light" (Genesis 1:3), and there was light. He spoke the universe into existence. He is great in power, in wisdom, and in wealth.

I do not really understand why God loves us. But His love for us is all the more mysterious when we realize that we are sinners. Romans 3:10 says, "There is none righteous, no, not one." Romans 3:23 adds, "For all have sinned, and come short of the glory of God."

Anyone can love someone who is lovable. But it takes a special kind of love to love someone who is offensive. Our sin is more offensive to God than we could ever know, but Romans 5:8 says, "God commendeth his love toward us, in that, while we were yet sinners, Christ died for us."

The Bible teaches that our ways are not God's ways. We have all gone astray like lost sheep (Isaiah 53:6). We have rebelled against God and His ways. Our thoughts are not like God's thoughts. Our eyes have been dimmed, our ears dulled, our minds twisted, our hearts depraved. And yet the fact is that God loves us.

Some time ago I was preaching in Berlin, Germany. Many came to profess faith in Christ at the close of the service. A young man from the United States Air Force came to me. He was stationed in Germany. He poured out to me a sordid story of sin and carelessness.

He said, "I come from a good home, and I have good parents, and I grew up in a sound church. I never dreamed I could do the things I have done."

I quoted to him from Jeremiah 17:9, "The heart is deceitful above all things, and desperately wicked: who can know it?" We should not be shocked to find out the sins that we are capable of, my friend. Every time I see a man or woman caught in some horrible, wretched sin, I think, *There but for the grace of God goes George Sweeting.*

My friend, the astounding thing is not the depth of sin into which a man can fall, but the depth of God's love to those of us guilty of such sin. And all of us are guilty. There is not one of us who has not lied, or cheated, or thought vile thoughts, or been guilty of hatred. All those things are as horrible to God as the worst thing you can think of.

Sin is contrary to God's very nature. It is abhorrent to Him. He is holy. He is pure. He is righteous. Our smallest sin is monstrous in His eyes.

And yet He loves us. That is indeed a mystery.

THE MAGNITUDE OF GOD'S LOVE

A second great truth I think of in connection with John 3:16 is the magnitude of God's love for us. He gave His only begotten Son!

Only a parent can understand the full import of those words. God's love was so great that He was willing to sacrifice His only begotten Son, the Lord Jesus, to pay for our sins.

The Lord Jesus was sinless. He had no guilt. He was not worthy of death. He was as deserving of the love of God as we are of God's wrath. Hebrews 4:15 says, "[He] was in all points tempted like as we are, yet without sin." Hebrews 7:26 says that He was "holy, harmless, undefiled, separate from sinners." Peter wrote that He "did no sin, neither was guile found in his mouth" (1 Peter 2:22). John wrote, "In him is no sin" (1 John 3:5). Even a centurion at His crucifixion, seeing the way he died, "glorified God, saying, Certainly this was a righteous man" (Luke 23:47).

But 2 Corinthians 5:21 says, "For he hath made him to be sin for us, who knew no sin, that we might be made the righteousness of God in him."

"Made him to be sin for us"! It is impossible for a mortal mind fully to grasp the complete truth of that statement, I'm sure. How could the eternal, sinless Son of God be made *sin* for us?

The apostle Paul is saying in that verse that in the hours our Lord hung on that cross, He was bearing our sin and taking the punishment for it. In those awful hours, the wrath of God the Father was poured out on God the Son!

Have you ever wondered why, hanging from the cross, the Son of God cried, "My God, my God, why hast thou forsaken me?" (Matthew 27:46). It was because in that hour, as He hung there bearing our sins, God the Father had to turn His back on God the Son, because He was bearing our sin.

Galatians 3:13 says, "Christ hath redeemed us from the curse of the law, being made a curse for us: for it is written, Cursed is every one that hangeth on a tree." He was cursed for our sakes!

Do you want to see a demonstration of the love of God, my friend? Look at Christ on the cross. See His love for us. That is the profoundest picture of the love of God.

There is nothing God would not do for us. He has already given His most precious possession—His own Son. Romans 8:32 says, "He that spared not his own Son, but delivered him up for us all, how shall he not with him also freely give us all things?"

Yes, my friend, God's love is great in its depth. But it is great in its scope as well. Whom does God love? Sinners. Which sinners? All of them. "For God so loved the *world*," it says. The whole world! God's love is for you, my friend, no matter who you are.

No matter how much you have sinned, God loves you. No matter what color your skin is, God loves you. Your nationality does not matter. Your economic class does not matter. How you look does not matter. How you have acted does not matter. God loves you!

God's love is truly a marvelous thing.

THE MEANING OF GOD'S LOVE

The third great truth I think about whenever I read John 3:16 is the truth of the meaning of God's love.

In D. L. Moody's day, the love of God was not a widely known concept. Preachers preached sermons about God's wrath. God was thought of as an angry being, anxious to squash sin and wipe out sinners. The widespread view of God was much like my childhood picture of a judge sitting on a throne.

Largely because of D. L. Moody's ministry and the influence of his preaching, the message that God is love became more widely known. But many have a warped understanding of the truth.

God is love, but that does not mean that He is tolerant of sin. He hates sin. But he loves the sinner. He has paid the price to redeem us from our sins. But He will judge those who reject the Lord Jesus.

My friend, never get the idea that because God is love He will overlook our sins. Don't think that because God is love we can ignore His Word or trifle with spiritual things and have Him simply wink at it. He still hates sin. He still demands obedience. He still requires repentance. He still deserves our reverance and worship and submission.

But because God is love, we can be assured that He will forgive the repentant sinner—not because he ignores the sin, but because the sin has already been paid for.

And that is the real meaning of God's love. He has made atonement for our sins. He has paid the price. He offers forgiveness and salvation and a fresh start to those who will trust Him.

Look again at John 3:16. And notice two sets of three words, "Believeth in him," and "should not perish." What does it mean to believe in Him? It means more than simply accepting the facts about Him. It means to trust in Him, to commit one's life to Him, to cast oneself completely on Him in faith. It is a faith that results in action, according to James. It is a life-changing experience, according to Paul.

Have you had such an experience? Have you put your faith in Christ to transform your life, to save you from your sins? If you are still trying to free yourself from your sins, or if you are trying to please God by the "goodness" of your life, then you have never really trusted Him in this way.

Look at those other three words, "should not perish." We deserve to perish. The wages of sin is death. We have sinned. We should die. The Lord Jesus did not deserve to perish, and yet He died on the cross. He has paid the price. There is no need for you and me to die. He offers us everlasting life, and it is a gift that He has bought and paid for.

Perhaps you fear death. There is nothing so fearful as the thought of dying with the uncertainty of what lies beyond the grave. But God's Word says that "whosoever believeth in him should not perish." He gives eternal life. There is nothing to fear, if we have trusted Him. God is love.

John 3:18 says, "He that believeth in him is not condemned: but he that believeth not is condemned already, because he hath not believed in the name of the only begotten Son of God."

Into which category do you fall? It is all so simple; there

is no need to stumble over it. God offers eternal life as a gift. We may receive it through faith in the Lord Jesus. Or we may neglect it, do nothing, and thereby condemn ourselves.

God is love. It is not His will that any of us should perish. He has paid the price so that we need not be condemned. But by unbelief we can condemn ourselves.

My friend, what will you do with the Lord Jesus Christ? He loves you. He has already proved His love to you by bearing your sins on the cross. Will you trust Him completely right now and be freed from your sins? Will you respond to the love of God?

13

What Is Life?

Throughout history man has attempted to find the answer to the question "What is Life?" His search has taken him to every corner of the earth and even to the planets above. And yet, today many people are just as confused, just as uncertain as ever. To them the meaning of life remains a mystery, an unsolved and unsolvable riddle.

Let me suggest five possible answers to the meaning of life. Each of these is an answer that will, obviously, affect a person's whole philosophy and behavior. How do you view life?

LIFE IS A VEXATION

The first view, held by many people in our busy world, is that life is a vexation. It is a burden with which each of us is saddled. It is filled with problems, and little else.

Someone has called life "the predicament that precedes death." Life begins with a cry and ends with a groan, and that is about all some people see to it.

This is the view of the Hindus. They believe that life is simply a thing to endure. Did you ever wonder why there is so much suffering and starvation in the Hindu countries?

Partly it is because Hindus feel that it is of no value to help those who suffer, since each person must endure a certain amount of suffering anyway. They believe that to help a person who is suffering is to cause him to have to suffer more in the next life. They feel that, as a man is reincarnated, he moves up a step or so each time, according to how much he endured in the last lifetime.

Life, they believe, is merely a vexation, something to be endured. What a pessimistic view of life!

But there is some truth to the view that life is a vexation. Job 5:7 says, "Man is born to trouble, as the sparks fly upward." Life is not easy.

Why is life so hard? Because of man's sin. God's original intention for man was that he should have a life of peace and fullness. God created Adam and Eve and put them in a perfect environment. Everything that God had made was good. It was theirs to enjoy. Life for them was a pleasure.

But they rebelled against God. They sinned and brought a curse upon themselves and all of creation. Pain, sorrow, sweat, and toil were some of the results of that curse. Death was another result. Adam and Eve suffered the sorrow of seeing one child murdered and another become a murderer. Life was no longer a pleasure.

My friend, everything in life that is unpleasant is a result of man's sin. That is why life can sometimes seem like a vexation. Sin is the reason we all suffer heartaches and pain and disease and sorrow.

But there is more meaning to life than that. To say that life is simply a vexation and nothing more or less is a shortsighted view of things. God has a purpose for us in life.

LIFE IS A VOID

Others would say that life is simply a void—a big nothing. You might remember a popular song released several years ago by singer Peggy Lee entitled "Is That All There

Is?" In that song, she reached a conclusion that expressed the futility sensed by millions of people today. As she sings her plaintive tune, she recalls the memorable moments of her life—a childhood thrill at the circus, the ecstasy of falling in love—the times that stood out in her mind above all others. In her experience she sensed that something was missing, and she came to the unfortunate conclusion that life is a void.

If that's all there is to life, she concluded, "Let's break out the booze and have a ball."

What an expression of despair! And yet today millions of people give mental assent to those words, and other practice them as a life philosophy.

Matthew Arnold pictured the same kind of futility in his poem "Rugby Chapel":

> What is the course of the life
> Of mortal men on the earth?
> Most men eddy about
> Here and there—eat and drink,
> Chatter and love and hate,
> Gather and squander, are raised
> Aloft, are hurl'd in the dust,
> Striving blindly, achieving
> Nothing; and then they die—

James G. Hunker cynically said, "Life is like an onion—you peel off layer after layer and then you find that there is nothing to it."

In Shakespeare's *MacBeth,* the main character obeys his evil desires and murders the king. That leads to a succession of evil deeds. He becomes king, as he had schemed to do, but finds emptiness in the fulfillment of his desires. Shortly before his death he declares his view of life. "It is," he says, "a tale told by an idiot, full of sound and fury, signifying nothing."

What a tragic, tragic way to see life. And yet, my friend, outside of Jesus Christ, no other view is reasonably possible. There is no meaning to life apart from Him.

Suicide is on the increase in our nation. And the disturbing thing is the high rate of suicides among young people eighteen years of age and younger. The idea that life is merely a void is one of the contributing factors to this phenomenon. If life is empty, meaningless, why continue with it? Why not end it? Are we not better off dead then trapped in a meaningless existence?

But that, too, is a faulty view of life. Life is not a void. It can have real meaning. We were created for a purpose. And we can realize the fulfillment of that purpose in Jesus Christ.

LIFE IS A VACATION

A view of life that many in our world hold is that life is a vacation. Life is a time to have all the fun you can have. A popular beer commercial has for years proclaimed that since you only go around once, you should grab all the gusto you can.

It seems that our nation is caught up with this view of life. We spend more money on entertainment than on any other single item. We live in a pleasure-mad world.

This view of life is a rejection of responsibility. It is closely aligned with the attitude so prevalent in our nation that the world owes us everything.

The tragic thing about thinking of life as merely a vacation is that, while it sounds so good and promises so much, it proves to be a very empty way of life. Pleasure becomes drudgery. Things that once were thrilling and exciting become empty and boring.

I do not say that there is no pleasure in sin. On the contrary, sin can be enjoyable, but that enjoyment is short-lived. The thrill of sin becomes a crushing burden. Poet Robert Burns expresses quite well the brevity of pleasure.

> Pleasures are like poppies spread,
> You seize the flower,
> Its bloom is shed.
> Or like a snowfall on a river,
> A moment white, then gone forever.

And that is the problem with looking at life as merely a vacation. Pleasures do not satisfy. Sin does not fulfill—it only makes the desire greater and more difficult to satiate. Sin arouses the appetite for more sin. And the fleeting pleasures of sin are quickly forgotten.

There is no hope in such a life-style. What looks and sounds like so much fun and excitement is in reality empty. Instead of a vacation, it becomes enslavement.

LIFE IS A VAPOR

A fourth view of life is that it is a vapor. That is a scriptural way of looking at life. James asks, "What is your life? It is even a vapour, that appeareth for a little time, and then vanisheth away" (James 4:14).

Amidst all the uncertainty about life, one thing is certain, and that is that life is short. An interesting Bible study is to make a survey of the metaphors the Bible uses about life. There are eighteen of them, and they all refer to the fact that life is short.

Job says, "My days are swifter than a weaver's shuttle" (Job 7:6). And again, "My life is wind" (Job 7:7).

The psalmist compares our life to a fading flower or falling leaf. "As for man, his days are as grass: as a flower of the field, so he flourisheth. For the wind passeth over it, and it is gone; and the place thereof shall know it no more" (Psalm 103:15-16).

The writer of Chronicles records for us the words of

David: "Our days on earth are as a shadow, and there is none abiding" (1 Chronicles 29:15).

Psalm 90:9 says, "We spend our years as a tale that is told."

Life is short. Someone has said that the wood of the cradle rubs against the marble of the tomb. There is no question about it—the days of our lives pass very swiftly.

That does not mean that life is unimportant. When the Bible acknowledges the brevity of life, it is not saying that all is futility. Life is indeed short, but that is not a reason for despair.

LIFE IS A VICTORY

The ultimate view of life given to us in the Bible is that life is a victory. Romans 5:17 says that it is God's intention that "they which receive abundance of grace and of the gift of righteousness shall reign in life by one, Jesus Christ."

God wants us to reign in life! We are to live like kings. We are to be victorious. We are to see life as a victory, not a defeat.

How can we live life as a victory? I think Romans 5:17 suggests answers to that question.

First, it is "by one, Jesus Christ." God does not ask us to be victorious in our own power! He does not say, "Do the best you can; break all your bad habits; free yourself from your sin; clean up your life; and you will know victory." If we had the ability to do those things, victory would not be a problem.

No, my friend, victory does not come through our personal effort and striving. The way of victory in life may surprise you. God's way of victory in life for us is the way of death!

Death? Yes, not physical death, but death to self. Jesus said, "Except a corn of wheat fall into the ground and die, it abideth alone: but if it die it bringeth forth much fruit. He that loveth his life shall lose it; and he that hateth his life in this world shall keep it unto life eternal" (John 12:24-25). He urged His followers to take up a cross—an instrument of death!

Paul understood what the Lord Jesus meant. He wrote, "I am crucified with Christ: nevertheless I live; yet not I, but Christ liveth in me" (Galatians 2:20).

The answer to victory is found in simply dying to self and letting the Lord Jesus Christ take over our lives and live in and through us. He is always victorious.

A second secret of victory in Romans 5:17 is in those words "abundance of grace." God's grace is sufficient, but it goes even beyond that. His grace to us is abundant!

God, in His abundant grace, can enable us to be victorious in any circumstance in life. One of the most precious promises in all of the Word of God is 1 Corinthians 10:13, "There hath no temptation taken you but such as is common to man: but God is faithful, who will not suffer you to be tempted above that ye are able; but will with the temptation also make a way to escape, that ye may be able to bear it."

God, in His grace, promises to protect us from any insurmountable temptations. He will give us the power to say *no* to every temptation that Satan can hurl at us. He will not test us above our ability to endure. He wants us to be victorious!

Yes, my friend, His grace is abundant. But the key to experiencing victory in life is to understand that victory is available only to those who have received God's gift of eternal life. God's abundant grace and the power of the indwelling Christ are, according to Romans 5:17, companion gifts with the gift of life.

Have you been born again? Have you received God's gift of eternal life? If not, you can never see life as a victory. The means of victory in life are available only in Jesus Christ, and we must come to Him in faith.

Will you trust Christ today and know the freedom of living life as a victory? The apostle Paul said, "For to me to live is Christ" (Philippians 1:21). The victorious life begins when we allow the Lord Jesus Christ to come in and take over. Will you trust Him today and begin to enjoy that victory?

14

God's Favorite Word: *Come*

Jesus said, "Heaven and earth shall pass away: but my words shall not pass away" (Mark 13:31). Every word spoken by God is important and worthy of our most careful attention. They are all significant, but none is more significant than the one I've chosen to call "God's favorite word."

The word of which I'm thinking is a special word, a personal word, a word of invitation. It is the word *come.*

No one, of course, fully knows the mind of God. But it is my feeling that this word *come* is special to God because of the way it is used in the Scriptures.

A WORD SPOKEN WITH FREQUENCY

First, *come* is a word spoken with frequency. It is the word that God spoke to man before He judged the earth with the Flood. It is the same word that changed Simon from a rugged and coarse fisherman into Peter, a devoted disciple of the Lord Jesus Christ. It is the word that Jesus spoke to the little children that gathered about Him. He spoke it to the sick and burdened multitudes.

The hands of the Lord Jesus are always outstretched, open. To the weary He offers rest and comfort. "Come to me, all ye that labor and are heavy laden," said our Lord in Matthew 11:28, "and I will give you rest."

The hands of Christ are outstretched and open to lift the fallen, to bless the children, to touch the sick, and to save the lost.

Consider the account of Noah found in Genesis 6-8. The earth was corrupt, much as it is today. The Lord saw that every imagination of man's heart was only evil continually. The world was in bad shape. So the Lord decided to destroy it.

It was under those circumstances that God spoke the first recorded use of the word *come*. It was an invitation to salvation to Noah and his whole family (see Genesis 7:1).

In the midst of evil and judgment and destruction, God spoke in compassion and grace, and the word He used was *come*.

Throughout the Bible we find God's invitation to come for forgiveness and salvation. In fact, the word *come* is found more than six hundred times throughout the Bible.

A WORD SPOKEN WITH CLEMENCY

And *come* is almost always a word spoken with clemency. From the first time God said "come" to Noah and his family, through the last occurrence of the word in the final chapter of the book of Revelation, God spoke the word *come* in mercy and grace and forgiveness.

Think with me for a moment about Christ's confrontation with the blind beggar Bartimaeus. In Luke 18 we are told of this interesting encounter.

It was probably a beautiful morning in Jericho, and blind Bartimaeus found a warm, sunny spot against a wall where he would be sure to meet many people. But soon he began to hear the hum of many voices and the shuffling of feet. His trained ears told him that this was not the usual crowd of passers by.

Luke 18:36 tells us that, "hearing the multitude pass by, he asked what it meant." He was told that it was Jesus of Nazareth passing by. Bartimaeus had heard of Him! And he knew the Lord's reputation for doing miracles.

"Jesus, thou Son of David," he cried, "have mercy on me" (v. 38).

And although those who stood by him began to rebuke him and push him out of the way, he pushed forward. Something within him must have told him that it was now or never. He knew that this might be his only opportunity to meet Jesus. He began to cry more loudly.

Verse 40 tells us Jesus' response. "Jesus stood, and commanded him to be brought unto him." Can you hear the compassion in the Savior's voice as He says to Bartimaeus, "Come"? Can you see the love in this One who reaches beyond the shouts of the crowd to call a poor, blind beggar?

The Lord Jesus stopped. He paused where He was and called for Bartimaeus. This was the Omnipotent One, reaching out to meet the need of a beggar. The Lord asked, "What wilt thou that I shall do unto thee?" (v. 41).

Notice how Bartimaeus replied. He did not ask for money. He did not request new clothing. He did not ask for power or for wealth. He simply said, "Lord, that I may receive my sight" (v. 41).

And the Lord Jesus gave him what he asked for.

My friend, the Lord Jesus says, "Come." He is not calling us for judgment but for mercy. He calls us with love and compassion. He calls us to trust Him. He calls us to take His yoke upon us, but His yoke is easy and His burden is light (see Matthew 11:29-30). He promises us rest.

A WORD SPOKEN WITH URGENCY

More than anything else, I want you to notice that *come* is a word spoken with urgency. Bartimaeus understood that. He wanted to meet the Lord Jesus right away. And it was a good thing he did, too. The Lord Jesus never returned to Jericho. That turned out to be the only opportunity Bartimaeus would ever have had to meet the Savior.

Luke 19 tells about another encounter the Lord Jesus had in Jericho. While He was there, great crowds of people thronged around Him. Because of the masses of people, a little man named Zacchaeus decided to climb up into a tree to get a better view of the Savior. In verse 5 we read that "when Jesus came to the place, he looked up, and saw him, and said unto him, Zacchaeus, make haste, and come down; for today I must abide at thy house."

"Come," said Jesus. "Make haste . . . to day." Can you hear the urgency in His voice? There is not much time.

The Lord speaks with tender, loving compassion, but He speaks with urgency. Do you remember the account of the destruction of Sodom and Gomorrah? Lot was warned that God would destroy the city. He was told to take his family and flee. But he delayed. He waited.

Genesis 19:16 says, "And while he lingered, the men [who were angelic messengers] laid hold upon his hand . . . the LORD being merciful unto him: and they brought him forth, and set him without the city." The Lord was merciful to Lot. The angels took Lot and his family by the hand, and led them out of the city.

But Lot still delayed. Verse 22 tells us that God told him, "Haste thee, escape thither; for I can not do any thing till thou be come thither." "Come," said God, and He said it with urgency. But He was waiting.

God cannot be mocked. He does not wait forever. You know what happened. As they were leaving, Lot's wife turned back to look. It was a fatal mistake. The Bible tells us that "she became a pillar of salt" (Genesis 19:26).

My friend, God is patient. Second Peter 3:9 says, "The Lord is not slack concerning his promise, as some men count slackness; but is longsuffering to us-ward, not willing that

any should perish, but that all should come to repentance."
There is that word again, *"come."*

When David Brainerd, the great missionary statesman, was seventeen years old, he was confused about God's plan of salvation. He knew that the Bible told him to come to Christ, but he didn't know how to come. He said, "I thought I would gladly come to Jesus, but I had no directions as to getting through."

As he prayed, Brainerd thought, *When a mother tells her child to come to her, she does not tell him how to come. He may come with a run, a skip, a jump, or a bound. He may come crying or singing or shouting. It doesn't matter how he comes, so long as he comes.*

My friend, it doesn't matter how you come to Christ. The important thing is that you do come. We sing a song in the church:

> Just as I am, without one plea,
> But that Thy blood was shed for me—
> And that thou bid'st me come to Thee.
> O Lamb of God, I come, I come.*

People of all kinds came to the Lord Jesus. Bartimaeus was a poor, blind beggar. Nicodemus was a ruler of the Jews. The woman at the well was a Samaritan. Zacchaeus was a tax collector. Jesus accepted all people who came to Him in repentance and faith. He accepted publicans and prostitutes, Pharisees and lepers. He ministered to Jews and Gentiles, men and women, slaves and free men.

My friend, no matter who you are, no matter what your circumstances are, the Lord Jesus invites you to come.

How should we come? Come with a repentant heart. The Lord Jesus said, "They that be whole need not a physician, but they that are sick. . . . I am not come to call the righteous, but sinners to repentance" (Matthew 9:12-13).

---

*Charlotte Elliott, 1834.

Read the New Testament. Many people came to the Lord Jesus; the only ones who turned away from Him were those who came to Him without a sense of their own need.

Matthew 19:16-24 tells of a wealthy young man who came to Jesus and asked what he could do to get eternal life. The account tells us that he went away from Jesus sad. Why? The beggars and sinners that came to Him never went away sad. He taught that He could give life to those who would come to Him. What was wrong?

Look closely at the passage, and you will see. The young man had no genuine sense of his own need. He felt that he had everything that he needed. When the Lord Jesus told him that he should keep the commandments, the young man's response was, "All these things have I kept from my youth up: what lack I yet?" (v. 20).

"What do I need?" he asked. "I have kept all the law. I am not a sinner."

There was nothing the Lord Jesus could do for him. My friend, we must come to the Lord Jesus with a deep sense of need. He came not to call the righteous, but sinners unto repentance. And all of us have sinned.

How should we come? Come believing. Faith is the ingredient He is looking for. A Gentile woman came to Jesus looking for deliverance for her daughter. Unlike the rich man, she was filled with a sense of her own need. And she would not be put off. The Lord Jesus said several things to her that would have discouraged most people, but she was insistent. Finally He said to her, "O woman, great is thy faith: be it unto thee even as thou wilt" (Matthew 15:28). She was rewarded for her faith.

My friend, Your good works mean nothing to God; it is your faith that He wants to see. Isaiah 64:6 says, "All our righteousnesses are as filthy rags."

On the other hand, Hebrews 11:6 says, "He that cometh

to God must believe." Salvation is by grace through *faith*. God is looking for your faith.

The very last chapter in the Bible is a wonderful appeal to each of us. God is saying, "Come." Revelation 22:17 says, "And the Spirit and the bride say, Come. And let him that heareth say, Come. And let him that is athirst come. And whosoever will, let him take the water of life freely."

The invitation is open. It is an invitation to life. It is an invitation for you. God is saying, "Come," to whosoever will. Someone has taken the word *come* and made an acrostic. *C* is for children; *O* is for the old; *M* is for middle-aged; *E* is for everyone. God is calling you to come.

My friend, won't you come today and drink freely of the water of life that He has promised?

Moody Press, a ministry of the Moody Bible Institute, is designed for education, evangelization, and edification. If we may assist you in knowing more about Christ and the Christian life, please write us without obligation: Moody Press, c/o MLM, Chicago, Illinois 60610.